Cancer's Gifts With Love & Hope

To Russ,
Love & hope,
Barb Neff —

Cancer's Gifts With Love & Hope

Robert V. Heffernan

iUniverse, Inc.
Bloomington

Cancer's Gifts With Love & Hope

iUniverse books may be ordered through booksellers or by contacting:

iUniverse
1663 Liberty Drive
Bloomington, IN 47403
www.iuniverse.com
1-800-Authors (1-800-288-4677)

ISBN: 978-1-4759-9060-7 (sc)
ISBN: 978-1-4759-9061-4 (ebk)

Printed in the United States of America.

iUniverse rev. date: 5/15/2013

*Names of most patients used in this book have
been changed to protect their privacy.*

*Names of medical professionals are their real names,
because they deserve public recognition
for their amazing work.*

Table of Contents

Foreword

AT 9:30 ON A Wednesday night in the ninth floor medical oncology unit at Yale-New Haven Hospital, an IV pole next to my bed drips rapidly into a PICC line inserted in my upper right arm.

The TV drones on but it's hard to get interested in a program. I am so nauseous in this second week of Interleukin-2 treatment. I've put on some 18 pounds of fluid weight. My hands and face are swollen. My skin has a terrible rash and itches like hell. Not only is it hard to sleep feeling so lousy, the Yale staff has to wake me up every two hours to take my blood pressure and temperature.

Right now, cancer is looking real ugly to me.

The drug is ramping up my immune system so much that it's turning on my own body. Lacking any other effective treatments, the Yale doctors have said if IL-2 doesn't work, everything else is experimental from here on out. I know the odds, and they are not pretty. Less than eight per cent will get a "complete response", a remission. But it's the last FDA-approved treatment for my cancer. 100 years from now, I'm thinking, this will look so barbaric to future medical practitioners. They're hyper-activating my whole immune system in the hopes it will somehow attack the cancer as an invader.

An hour earlier, I ordered my Mom and my husband Allen to go home. Throughout my three-year ordeal with cancer, they have stood vigil out of unconditional love. I can see the worry and fear in their faces. It pains me to see what my disease is doing to them.

Several good friends and loved ones have also come to visit. Kind of strange for them to see me like this. Two nights earlier, one visitor fled apologetically when at the precise moment he arrived my body went into the rigors—uncontrollable violent shaking. I shook the recliner chair so hard one of the screws went ka-ching across the room. A nurse injected two doses of Demorol to calm the tremors.

Cancer is looking quite ugly to them, too. But the seasoned professionals who are treating me have seen it before many times, over and over.

A few weeks after I returned home, the bills started arriving. Charges for the first week of Interleukin-2 treatment totaled over $136,000. Charges for the second week: $152,000. All I did was lay in bed hooked up to an IV pole—no surgery, no machines. A quarter of a million dollars for one cancer treatment that I would learn six weeks later did not work. The tumors kept growing anyhow.

The high cost of cancer looks ugly to society as a whole.

Yet, inside and outside my hospital room, goodness reigns. For all the pain and suffering that cancer has lobbed at me, I have seen so many beautiful aspects of this terrible disease.

I get up out of bed and force myself to walk the halls of the ninth floor, wheeling my IV pole with me. Despite feeling so sickly and weak, the walk comforts me with all the wonderful things I see.

From the floor's waiting room, I've been watching an army of construction workers building a monument to cancer's defeat: the new 14-story cancer hospital costing more than half a billion dollars. Thousands of people have come forward to contribute money for this amazing new building attached to Yale-New Haven. It'll be named after Joel Smilow, a businessman and philanthropist who gave Yale much of the total cost of the project.

This is all for people like me, I am thinking, as I gaze out the window way down to the first floor and back up to the top. I get choked up at the thought.

Walking back towards my room, I smile and cheer on cancer's biggest enemy—the medical teams who've chosen cancer fighting as a career. There's Mike Droniak, the handsome young nurse. So many other avocations he could have chosen, I guess, but he chose oncological nursing with such mixed outcomes. All cancer patients are fortunate he made that choice. There's Dr. Ruth Halaban who came to visit me, a lifelong Yale cancer researcher who not only is tinkering with my cancer cells, she's also mapped out my genome. There's my oncologist, Dr. Harriet Kluger, whom I think is the best at what she does. There's Sheila Turner APRN, who's been coordinating my in-patient treatment these two weeks. There's the social worker assigned to my case, Nora Rightmer, who helps hundreds of cancer patients just deal with it all. At least another 30 Yale staffers are working for me—Bob Heffernan, the cancer patient—doing lab tests, scans, surgery, billing, room maintenance, and on and on.

The true wonder of it all amazes me. The institution itself—Yale—is a bastion of medicine, symbolizing the persistent drive of humankind to quell disease and heal.

In every room on this floor, there are dozens of beautiful stories: one patient after another has chosen to fight cancer. Their personal battles and support from loved ones provides so much inspiration and respect. "Let me know who else has my cancer on the floor, I'd love to chat with them," I tell my nurses. I've quickly learned how special is the bond between patients.

One out of every four Americans will get cancer sometime in their lifetime, says the American Cancer Society. The odds are great the disease in some way will have touched everyone reading this book. We all know somebody who has been treated for cancer. We know far too many who've lost their battle.

Nobody knows more than I how bad cancer is. This book will not sugarcoat the disease. Instead, it's really a story about how we can find goodness and beauty in even the most terrible things life throws at us. Cancer is all about the intimate human experience. It brings out the best traits in so many of us. How we choose to handle a disease is just that—a *choice*. We live with cancer, beat back cancer, or sadly succumb to cancer.

I have chosen to focus on *Cancer's Gifts*, and the love and hope that go with them.

Composure

My mind raced as I sat inside the examination room. The wait for Dr. Loyd Godwin dragged on. I felt a sense of fate and foreboding in the air.

After all, how bad could it be?, I consoled myself. It could be *nothing*. And if it's *something*, then it's just skin cancer and they'll take care of it. You're in a dermatologist's office, for Christ sakes, I thought. Who ever died from a visit to the *dermatologist*?

Then my thoughts went self-critical. You waited too long, you *idiot*. You felt that little bump on top of your scalp back in November, and you waited until mid-January to make a doctor's appointment. Silently, I nodded agreement with myself in the privacy of the exam room.

Suddenly, a knock on the door, and in walked a young woman, one of Dr. Godwin's assistants. "What are you here for today?," she asked.

"Biopsy results," I answered stiffly.

She flipped through the file folder on the counter. Her eyes didn't look up.

"Hmmm," she hummed lowly. "The doctor will be in to see you shortly."

Like all patients, I tried to read her body language. That wasn't good. She didn't even look at me. What did that file tell her? Looked like she couldn't get out of the room fast enough. Oh-oh, I thought. My stomach tightened with that tension all patients feel before getting *the results*.

She left me to sit another longish period of time. Just two weeks earlier in the same room, Dr. Godwin had scooped the bump, lump, whatever it was off the top of my balding scalp. At one point in the process, he inadvertently blurted out, "What is it?"

That was clue number one I might be in trouble. An experienced dermatologist had not seen this before. *Calm your ass down*, I ordered myself. Whatever it is, you'll just have to handle it.

After what seemed an eternity, another knock on the door. This one was louder, from the Doctor himself.

Dr. Godwin's usual smile, rushed persona, and loud voice were missing. He walked over near me, sat on a stool. For a brief moment, I saw a tightness, a seriousness in his face.

"Bob, I have to tell you this came back from the lab as a malignant melanoma."

"It's very serious. I'm sorry to have to tell you that."

All at once, I felt flush, like my blood pressure had both spiked and fallen simultaneously—something I had never felt before. I remember swallowing hard. I stiffened my back.

"I'm sending you to Yale," the Doctor said.

Holy crap, I thought. This really is *serious*. He's sending me to *Yale*. Every state, every nation has their blue ribbon hospitals that handle the most serious medical conditions. Yale-New Haven Hospital was one of those revered institutions.

"Here's what's going to happen….," the Doctor began ticking off what lay ahead of me. The head of Yale's melanoma program, Dr. Stephan Ariyan, a gifted plastic surgeon, would remove a wide area of scalp tissue—they call it *taking margins*—in an effort to collect any remaining cancer cells. Dr. Ariyan would also perform numerous tests and biopsies to see if the cancer had spread into the lymph system, which melanoma is known for.

I tried to act stoic and calm. Numbness came over me, as if my body released endorphins to deal with the bad news. *Focus*, you have to hear all of this, I ordered myself.

"I've checked and they all accept your insurance," Dr. Godwin assured me. "You've got a journey ahead of you, and the sooner you get this done the better. But hopefully the surgeon will get it all. They'll be monitoring you for several years."

Little did he know at the time just how incredible my fateful journey would become.

Leaving the doctor's office was a blur. Most cancer patients have the same experience. This is why nobody should get a cancer diagnosis alone. But it was my body, my problem, and I wanted to handle it first by myself, to prepare myself, digest the news, *compose* myself, get my bearings.

Walking back out past other patients in the waiting room,

I thought how lucky they were with their menial complaints of skins rashes and psoriasis, and desire for wrinkle-free skin with Botox. Few of them would suspect they could ever receive such a devastating diagnosis from a dermatologist as I just got. We each have our daily challenges, and they're all relative to our priorities, our fears, and our hopes.

Walking down the medical building staircase, walking up the parking lot, driving the car back to the office—the body went on autopilot as my mind grappled with how to handle this perceived threat to life.

The radio blared as I started the car. Click, off it went. I had to think this crisis over. How would I break the news to my Mom, to my life partner/husband Allen, to my friends, to my family, to my industry? As executive director of three state trade associations, I had not only a public-type job known by thousands of people, but also a huge responsibility that potentially could be interrupted by this.

When would I schedule the surgery and treatment? There were major conferences ahead requiring my management.

Did I have to tell anyone? A patient's right to medical privacy today is paramount. But if I didn't reveal my condition, there would be rampant rumors putting those close to me in difficult situations. And if I did open up, how much detail would I give out?

Would I be able to keep my jobs? Would I keep my health insurance? Would my associations keep me on the payroll? Would I be able to handle household bills?

Almost secondary to all of this came the unthinkable: this could actually kill me. The cancer could spread. The treatment could be painful. The suffering, the incapacity, the sadness, the uncertain future….. Gosh, I didn't even have a will yet.

Quickly, my brain recalled the many others in my life who had died of cancer. None of it was pretty. In fact, there were tortuous memories of loved ones who went through hell. But then I remembered how each of them managed to handle their crisis with grace to the very end. That was a calming thought.

This mountain of worry kept spiraling like a tornado inside my head on the 25-minute ride back to the office. Good thing we have a subconscious mind, because it was driving my car.

How cancer patients maintain their *composure* in face of shattering news is truly a beautiful human trait.

The first skill a cancer patient learns is *composing* himself/ herself when hit by the cancer sledgehammer. It's one of life's supreme tests that bring out the goodness in everyone.

Anger, denial, and fear are common emotions for the cancer warrior. "Why me, damn it?", or "This can't be happening to me!", or "Oh God, I'm afraid of what's going to happen."

Many patients break down in tears at the news they have cancer. They have every right to let it all out. In fact, it's probably therapeutic to cry. The only tears I have shed during my ordeal have come for joyous reasons. And let me tell you that tears of joy are just as cleansing and emotional as those of fright.

The majority of patients who hear the dreaded phrase, "You have cancer", react with calm and dignity, although our insides are an emotional wreck. The Puritan traits of our early American settlers show themselves when we're hit by cancerous news. We usually pull ourselves together, summon an inner strength we never knew we had, and march on to fight the disease arm-in-arm with our medical team. We're instinctively hopeful and optimistic.

Dealing with cancer is an emotional undertaking because we tend to associate cancer with impending death. The overall five-year relative survival rate for all cancer sites has been steadily improving with medical advances and early detection—from 49.3 percent in 1974-76 to about 60 percent today. So it's no wonder we patients struggle with composing ourselves as we endure treatment after treatment, and the anxiety of test results.

We want to live and enjoy life, just like everyone else. OK, maybe a little more than the rest of you.

The wait to hear lab results from my first surgery in March 2007 was a nerve-wracking 10 days.

The Yale surgeon, Dr. Stephan Ariyan, excised a gouge of tissue out of my scalp, an area of about three square inches, leaving a gaping hole that he promised would close naturally without leaving an ugly scar (a procedure he pioneered known as myocutaneous flap reconstruction).

While I lay under anesthesia in one of Yale's 38 operating rooms, Dr. Ariyan and his team awaited instant results from the lab on the biopsy sample he took from the lymph nodes in my left neck. Pathologists saw something they couldn't confirm as more melanoma, and needed to send it out for further testing. So they bandaged me up and sent me home—amazingly a one-day surgery. On the 75-minute drive home, I vomited—a side effect from the anesthesia.

My composure skills would be tested yet again in Dr. Ariyan's office 10 days later. I kept telling myself in the interim, with a hole like that in my head, he just *had* to have gotten all the cancer. As the good Doctor checked my bandages and complimented me on my scalp's healing progress, he softly dropped the big bomb: "The lab confirms some melanoma cells in one of the lymph nodes in your left neck. We need to remove that and as a precaution all the nodes there."

Whoa. A sinking feeling came over me. I looked at Allen and closed my eyes momentarily, exhaled long and slumped on the exam table. The cancer sledgehammer had been swung at me again.

Allen would take on the critical role of cancer patient caregiver. A medical technologist himself, he insisted that no longer would I go alone to any cancer appointment. Having him with me helped keep my composure and strength.

We left directly from the Doctor's office to a conference I had to attend in Newport, RI. On the drive up Interstate 95, we debated how to break this latest news to my Mom who lived in Vermont. My head still in bandages, I now had the chore of explaining my malady to business colleagues at the conference. I chose to put up the strong front: I've got one of the nation's best doctors working on this, and we're going to beat it.

In another two weeks, I was back at Yale for a more serious surgery, a radical neck lymphadenectomy. Dr. Ariyan cut a long incision that ran from behind my left ear, down the neck, and across the left shoulder. I went home with a tube coming out the front shoulder to drain lymph fluid for a week.

Doctors often expect emotional breakdowns when they deliver that diagnosis, "You have cancer." Not all medical students are fully trained in the optimum psychological deliverance of bad news, but they should. To be fair, neither are patients out there taking self-help seminars on how to respond to a cancer diagnosis before they know they have it. I certainly had no training and do not profess to be the expert.

The bedside manner of doctors, nurses, and other medical staff is key to how a patient deals with developments in any disease. When cancer patients get together, they inevitably swap stories of how their medical team "broke the news" to them. It's key to how a patient maintains his/her composure. It sets the stage for trust in the doctor-patient relationship, and for the long-term success or failure of the treatment.

First, deliverance of cancer treatment results requires that doctors and nurses understand how intensely emotional an experience it really is. There's a special knack to doing it right. One type of medical professional personality is all business: you have cancer, this is the treatment, any questions, get up and leave. That's cold, stiff, leaving no opening for emotion. Another type of a doctor's approach seems better suited for the cancer patient: a softer, slower, more compassionate, understanding touch where the doctor isn't aloof and insulating himself. Every cancer patient is so different and their response so unpredictable.

It's not an easy job for doctors and nurses to deliver results. Patients must understand that. Several times, I gave words of sympathy to *my doctors* after they gave *me* bad news. Few doctors expect to hear that from a patient. But put yourself in their shoes: what would *your* stomach feel like if *you* had to tell someone they were about to undergo a life-threatening procedure? Medical professionals have their own struggles with how they keep *their* composure. It gets really hard for them the closer they connect to their patients.

Second, the more information a doctor gives, the easier it is for the patient to compose himself or herself. Information today empowers most cancer survivors to feel in control and enhance their serenity. Information reassures and comforts, whereas the unknown sparks fear in the cancer patient's mind. It also raises the patient's respect for the doctor. Plus, in this information-swamped world of the Internet, too much irrelevant data can be found to scare cancer survivors (but most patients will go to the web anyhow).

Thirdly, sometimes our own intuition as patients helps us anticipate what's coming. As much as I tried to convince myself that little lump on top of my scalp could be something else, in reality part of my mind had figured out weeks before the doctor visit that it probably was cancer. That fear of learning the horrible truth and what comes with it prevents too many people from seeking help early. And with cancer, time often means the difference between cure and a long struggle. But that intuition helped me compose myself and lessen the shock. It was still a shock, nonetheless.

Dr. Godwin delivered the initial diagnosis to me about as perfectly as any doctor could. He took his time, respected my emotions, had the next steps all laid out, and gave me the information I needed. He enabled me to compose myself with dignity.

Composure is less important when a cancer patient gets *good* news. Go ahead, jump up and scream, "Hooray!" You're entitled to celebrate. I remember the time a Yale patient came out of the clinic exam room and said aloud to the 30 people within earshot in the waiting room, "Clean scans!" Everyone erupted into applause and cheers.

Cancer treatment is fraught with twists and turns. Patients must confront the unexpected result over and over, each time facing a new challenge. The good news is patients get better and better at managing their composure with more experience in dealing with the disease. It's not that devastating news gets any easier to accept; we just adapt to handling it with more grace, sensibility, and perspective.

By and large, the patient who adeptly manages his *composure* is better prepared to withstand all facets of cancer. In the process, he or she also sets an example for all of us to live by and honor.

Journey

THE MOMENT A DOCTOR says, "You have cancer", fasten your seat belt. Get ready for the ride of your life. And, it's a ride for *saving and savoring* your life.

I had no idea what really lay ahead. No cancer patient ever knows for certain his future. Neither do the doctors know. They can guess quite well, but they're never sure about a patient's destiny. Not even the good briefing that Dr. Godwin gave me when he made that 2007 diagnosis of melanoma would accurately predict where the cancer might take me for the next six-plus years.

Like most people, I love taking a journey. There's the excitement of seeing new places, meeting new people, and the adventure of venturing into areas unknown. There's the thrill of discovery. As many patients do, I spent hours at home researching anything and everything about my cancer on the Internet. Good information empowers patients, but sorting what's useful and accurate from what's not on the worldwide web is a challenge. I was looking for clues about where the disease might take me from the experience of others.

Strangely, after the initial shock of the diagnosis slowly

wore off, I began to feel kind of excited. There could be painful moments ahead, but something inside me wanted to attack this new challenge with gusto, much like hiking a new trail in the Hawaiian mountains. I had to be careful not to fall off the cliff, and enjoy the beautiful sights along the way.

I left Dr. Godwin's office knowing only that surgery and medical tests were ahead of me. He booked the trip for me much like a travel agent, but the rest was up to me.

He referred my case to one of the best melanoma surgeons, Dr. Stephan Ariyan. Luckily for me, the timing of my cancer coincided with the golden years of Dr. Ariyan—a gifted plastic surgeon with keen knowledge of melanoma in the twilight of his long career at Yale. Made sense to me: cancer of the skin being handled by a plastic surgeon. Dr. Ariyan was also the Director of the Melanoma Unit in the Yale Cancer Center.

It was up to me to make that first appointment with Dr. Ariyan. I scheduled it six weeks later in early March, timed to come after a big trade show and other events that required my management.

All of us are accustomed to being in total control of our daily journeys. To a large degree, we cancer patients have the right to steer the course of our own treatment. I had already made two big mistakes: waiting too long to see the dermatologist, and then waiting too long to put the medical gears in motion once I had the diagnosis.

Cancer was going to teach me some very big lessons

along the treatment highway. Lesson number one: run, don't walk, when cancer is involved.

Whenever Dr. Ariyan walked into the exam room or the operating room, I had the sensation of meeting the captain of a Boeing 747 jumbo jet. He commanded my respect with his calm intellect. I felt confident knowing this man would help steer my melanoma journey.

Before he operated on the top of my head to remove much scalp tissue—and hopefully, any cancer cells lingering after the initial biopsy—there were a battery of pre-surgical tests. One afternoon, a radiologist made several painful injections of a radioactive liquid into my scalp to figure out how lymph fluid flowed from the cancerous area. That would later guide the surgeon towards those lymph nodes in my neck that might possibly trap stray cancer cells. There were blood tests, and EKGs, and so on.

The day of my first surgery for cancer, I saw how the Yale staff similarly held Dr. Ariyan up on a pedestal. "He's the best, the most thorough surgeon," one anesthesiologist assured me after inserting an IV in a pre-op dressing room. Another good sign: Yale medical students lined up to observe Dr. Ariyan's techniques inside the operating room. He also served as professor of surgery in the Yale Medical School.

For most melanoma patients, the journey ends with the first surgery that removes the cancer before it has spread. They're simply monitored once or twice a year thereafter. But for me, the cancer had entered the lymph system, forcing Dr. Ariyan to schedule me for major surgery number two: removal of all lymph nodes in the left neck.

In the operating suite, Dr. Ariyan found one of the cancerous lymph nodes rested against the nerve in my neck, so he removed it, leaving the area permanently numb. I would have to go through life with little nerve feeling every time I turned my neck to look left. "Oh that's minor, I can live with it," I reassured my good Doctor when he checked on me the next morning in the hospital.

A cancer patient's medical journey is often dictated by what "stage" the person is in. The moment doctors found cancer in my lymph nodes, I entered the territory of stage three cancer. My chances of survival plummeted, according to the statistics.

The National Cancer Institute describes staging as the severity of a person's cancer based on the extent of the original (primary) tumor and whether or not cancer has spread in the body. Staging is important for several reasons:

- Staging helps the doctor plan the appropriate treatment.
- The stage can be used to estimate the person's prognosis.
- Knowing the stage is important in identifying clinical trials that may be suitable for a particular patient.

Stages 0, 1, and 2 are most curable. Stage 3 means a larger tumor size and/or spread of the cancer beyond the organ in which it first developed to nearby lymph nodes and/or organs adjacent to the location of the primary tumor.

Stage 4 is what I wanted to avoid most: metastasis in a distant organ where cure rates are lowest and mortality the highest.

⁂

Yale's melanoma team now knew I needed aggressive treatment, because the cancer was on the move. Melanoma cells have a sneaky reputation for leaving lymph nodes and entering the blood stream, then lodging in organs like the liver, lungs, and brain where they cause big trouble.

Experts say there are six cancers where progress has been the slowest and outcomes the most difficult: liver, lung, brain, pancreatic, esophageal/stomach, and—unlucky for me—my cancer, melanoma. To make matters worse, metastatic melanoma seldom responds to chemotherapy. And, in 2007, there were only a small handful of treatments approved by the Food and Drug Administration for melanoma.

Treatment for cancer patients is often determined by the *accepted medical practice* at that point in time, and consequently, whether their insurance will cover it. Here's where the patient's steering wheel often is commandeered by adopted protocols in effect at the moment. Many patients have to decide the path they'll follow, weighing such yucky things as side effects, toxicity, whether the treatment cures, prolongs, or even itself kills. Clinical trials of experimental treatments usually present more options.

My own options were few.

In his downtown New Haven office one week after the surgery, Dr. Ariyan pulled a drain hose out of my shoulder that had captured lymph fluid leftover from removal of the nodes in the neck.

"I've assigned Harriet Kluger to be your oncologist," he said while yanking sutures out of my skin. "She'll handle your treatment from now on….".

"But that means you're off my case?", I asked dejectedly. Dr. Ariyan's control made me feel so confident.

"If you need more surgery, she'll send you back to me," the Doctor responded businesslike.

My cancer was taking me down a new path. Never had an oncologist before. Never had a woman doctor either. Why couldn't Dr. Ariyan just handle whatever came next?

The medical world is segmented like the military. Patients normally start with their local doctors, then go to a specialist. From there, cancer patients routinely see a surgeon. The surgical corps branches out depending on where the cancer is located—lung cancer requires a thoracic surgeon, brain tumors require neurosurgeons, etc. Radiologists handle radiation-type treatments and interpret scans.

Then there are the *oncologists*: medical doctors that study and treat cancer and cancer patients. They can work with all types of cancers or just one. They are not necessarily surgeons but may advise during the surgery. They're like commanders in the process, overseeing and coordinating all the treatments that might include chemotherapy, radiation, and so on.

I could have found my own oncologist, but I trusted Dr.

Ariyan's judgment too much to question his decision. Trust is an essential linchpin in the cancer patient's treatment.

Harriet Kluger M.D. was part of the Yale melanoma team. It was an easy decision to stay the course and make the appointment.

❧   ❧

"I know *all* about you," Dr. Kluger said with a broad smile as she walked in my Yale exam room two weeks later. Those kind words immediately put me at ease.

I detected something like a British accent in her soft voice. She had grown up in South Africa and received her medical degree from Tel Aviv University in Israel.

"Call me Harriet," she said. We became fast friends. Her sweet personality enabled close relationships with her patients.

Only the stethoscope draped around her neck signaled that she was a doctor. For the next several years, I never saw her in the typical white lab coat. Harriet didn't need a uniform to convey her qualifications. Everything about her radiated a relaxed, keen medical intellect par none. The moment she spoke, you knew she was an outstanding professional.

Dr. Harriet Kluger, I would later learn, was as much a researcher as a doctor of cancer. She had many projects with brainy titles that were published in the medical literature, such as *C-Raf is Associated with Disease Progression and Inhibition of Apoptosis in a Subset of Melanomas*, or *Expression of sorafenib targets in melanoma patients treated with carboplatin, paclitaxel and sorafenib*. But talking to her one-on-one, you'd never get the impression she was such a scientist.

Like Dr. Ariyan, Harriet also taught in the Yale Medical School as an Associate Professor of Medical Oncology. She saw patients only two days a week in the clinic. The rest of her time was spent being a leading expert in the international melanoma community.

My confidence in my medical team shot way up. I had landed in the best possible place for treatment of my cancer.

⚜

"I want to start you on Interferon," Dr. Kluger proposed.

My surgeon forewarned me this was the likely next step. Harriet explained that Interferon had some success in preventing spread of melanoma, and was one of the only FDA-approved treatments for stage three patients.

Interferons are proteins made and released by host cells within our own bodies in response to the presence of pathogens—such as viruses, bacteria, or parasites—or cancerous tumor cells. They allow communication between cells to trigger the protective defenses of the immune system that theoretically eradicate pathogens or tumors.

"How successful is it?," I asked. Every cancer patient wants to know the odds.

"Response rates are as high as 15%," I heard her say. "Some studies show it helps, some show it doesn't."

"Response? Is that the same as *cure*?", I wondered.

Harriet stiffened slightly. We were getting into tough territory for oncologists, who know it's dangerous to be held to published statistics on a treatment's effectiveness. She explained that *response* meant a reduction in tumor size or no evidence of disease for a relatively short period of time.

The cure rates from Interferon—elimination of the cancer—were only in the single digit percentiles at best.

"Wow," I sighed from my perch on the exam table. Harriet began what would become her usual ritual of using her hands to feel my lymph nodes in my neck, underarms, and groin.

Here were my options. At that moment, the doctors could see no other cancer, but they warned it would probably show up again somewhere in the body. I could wait until that sad day, or I could take a chance on a tough treatment that might—just might—prevent a recurrence.

"So, let me get this straight," I said to Harriet. "We're going to rev up my immune system with Interferon in the hopes that it'll somehow recognize the cancer as an enemy and go after it?"

"Something like that," she smiled back.

Harriet explained the substance would be fed into my veins every day intravenously at high doses for the first month at Yale, then follow up with at-home injections of smaller doses for the next 11 months.

For the next entire year, I would feel like I had a bad case of the flu—every day.

"Ok, let's go for it," I said.

"From now on, we will watch you carefully," the good doctor predicted.

⚘   ⚘

The journey of cancer patients snags our loved ones along for the ride.

On the way home from Yale, Allen and I talked about how we would handle my year on Interferon. He had been with me every step of the way. In December 2005, our longtime relationship of love and respect became "legal" under Connecticut's new civil unions law for same sex couples. The staff at Yale thought it cool they could enter his name as my legal spouse in their computers. The new law made it clear he could speak for me when I couldn't.

"You're NOT driving back and forth from the treatments—I don't care WHAT you say," he demanded. "You're not going to do it, so don't even think…"

For the past four months, he had rearranged his life and work schedule to be with me during the surgeries and doctor's appointments. Fortunately, he drew blood every day from patients during his hospital lab work, so I would treasure a built-in technician to give me the at-home injections.

Cancer patients soon learn to let go their fear of needles.

The first Monday in June, I showed up at Yale's infusion center for cancer patients. It wasn't a pretty sight—some 30 reclining chairs with all sorts of toxic drugs dripping into the veins of people who had that look of enduring cancer therapy: bald heads, off-color skin, weight loss, the cast of illness.

Yet as I looked at each face, they flashed a smile. Sick as they were, they gave me a beautiful smile.

"Take any chair," a nurse motioned. I waved off quick thoughts of "what am I doing here", and "sure you want to go through with this."

Jen Piccirillo RN came over, introduced herself, and started opening an IV kit. She would become my buddy in the process. Tall, slender, athletic with long blonde hair, her broad smile welcomed me that first day of June 2007 to begin one year of Interferon treatments. In 20 days of intense high-dose treatment, her professionalism and confidence put me at ease. She missed a vein only once, and most times I hardly felt the needle stick. She had that gift. Over time, I would see the nurses in oncology as saints.

I decided to time these treatments in the afternoon, so I could work in the morning and rest earlier at night when the side effects would hit hardest.

For the first few days, I was amazed at how little the Interferon affected me. I dutifully brought my laptop and kept up with office work. But by Thursday and Friday of that first week, it started hitting me: nausea, tiredness, and a sickly feel all over. I had to force food down, and I couldn't taste it well. Diet Coke tasted like water. Sleeping and showering with an IV in the arm became a hassle.

On the way home from one of the treatments, I convinced Allen I felt good enough to drive. Just 30 minutes up the road, I nodded off at the wheel and almost hit a car in the other lane. It was only 5:00 in the afternoon. Interferon was exhausting me more than I knew.

By the second week of the daily infusions, I was asking for anti-nausea medicine. Zofran worked well, but it stopped up my bowels. At home, all I wanted to do was lay down on a couch or bed. By the third week, I was sleeping in the infusion chairs.

By the fourth week, my liver enzymes were screwy. Allen laughed hysterically when the melanoma nurse coordinator practically accused me of drinking alcoholic beverages during the treatment. I rarely drink. Three days before the end of June, Yale halted the Interferon. I had taken 18 days of the drug in very high doses. My labs told the doctors to stop and give my body a week off. First month of Interferon cost almost $54,000.

Yale set me up with at-home little needles at a much-reduced dosage. And for the next 11 months, I dutifully got injected three times a week. Cost per month: $4,000.

CT scans of my entire body and MRI scans of my brain, taken every three months, stayed clear of the cancer for the next year. But I felt flu-ish every day. I just toughed it out and hardly missed a day of work.

The last Interferon needle injections came one year later, Memorial Week 2008. I counted down the time, knowing good health would return within weeks of finishing the treatment. It had been a *long, long* year of feeling like crap every day. But this was my battle and I was determined to see it through. Allen and I celebrated with a four-day weekend in Cape Cod. Of course, he drove the car.

Ahhhh, to feel like normal again! Every cancer patient yearns for it. Crazy as it sounds, the treatment makes you feel sick, not the cancer. Every cancer therapy makes you appreciate good health. You know the old saying: when you've got your health, you've got *everything*.

By the last two weeks of June 2008, I was my old self again. Eating well. Sleeping normally. Life was good. Yale put my body through the scanner to check Interferon's effect.

I fidgeted nervously inside the exam room waiting for my July 2008 appointment with Dr. Kluger—now 16 months after the first diagnosis.

An APRN (nurse practitioner who ranks close to the doctor level in skills) walked in and smiled. That wasn't unusual, in fact APRNs are essential to the entire cancer treatment regimen.

This time she startled me by being the one to reveal how the scans turned out.

"Your scans look pretty good….."

Instantly my spirits rose.

"…But they show two nodules in the right lung measuring…"

I felt myself slump on the exam table with a loud exhale. Cancer was testing me yet again with a terrible diagnosis. But I quickly rebounded, took charge to take on the beast.

"Nodule?," I asked. "Could that be the cancer?" Never heard the term *nodule* before.

"Most likely, yes," she said, "but it could be something else too. Your previous scans don't show them."

Suddenly I became conscious of my breathing and my lungs. I felt nothing unusual and had not a clue that cancer could be there.

Moments later, Dr. Kluger walked in.

"Do you really think it's melanoma, in my *lung*?", I asked her point-blank.

Harriet made her head shake affirmatively up and down. She had seen it happen many times before with other melanoma patients.

"We think it should be removed with surgery," the Doctor advised.

Cancer has its own GPS system. Harriet would say, "Melanoma can show up anywhere in the body." And so can most other cancers, for that matter. Your body's circulatory system is actually an intricate system of highways—major arteries, veins, and capillaries. Cancer cells like to take off on their own journeys, hitchhiking the flow of blood and lymph fluid. Sometimes lodging randomly here and there, sometimes not.

All it takes is one, or two, or three miniscule cancer cells, travelling to form a metastasis.

Now I was in deep trouble, and I knew it. With that latest CT scan, I was officially in the perilous territory of cancer's last stage—Stage Four. The cancer was in a vital organ. From the National Cancer Institute came this frightening statistic: the median survival of patients with metastatic melanoma is 6–9 months with a 5-year survival rate of less than 5%.

Ironically, because I was feeling so perfect, Allen let me go to this appointment by myself. At our home in the Litchfield County hills, he was working in the flower garden when I got there.

"How did you make out?," he asked across the yard.

I shook my head and bit my lower lip. "It's in my lung."

He dropped his tool and rushed to hug me in a long emotional embrace in the warm setting sun of a July day. Surrounded by the beauty of maple trees and flowering plants, we both felt the preciousness of life in a moment of great apprehension.

~~~ ~~~

I'd never heard the word *thoracic* before, but there I was, being examined by Yale thoracic surgeon Frank Detterbeck MD.

The body's thoracic cavity (or chest cavity) houses your respiratory system (lungs), structures of the cardiovascular system (heart), and many structures of the digestive system, like the esophagus.

I didn't have lung cancer. I had a melanoma metastasis in the lung. There was an enormous difference. It behaved differently there and called for a whole other approach. But I still had to be treated by a lung specialist.

How ironic, I thought in the surgeon's exam room. My father smoked Lucky Strike cigarettes all his life and never got lung cancer. I never smoked and now had a cancer in my lung. Nobody ever said cancer was fair.

Among the best in his field, Dr. Detterbeck was also Yale Professor of Surgery, Chief of Thoracic Surgery, and Surgical Director of Thoracic Oncology. He intimately knew the innards of the human chest and especially the lungs.

Lung surgery scared me. Would I have to be on a respirator? Likely, only during surgery, the doctor assured me. Would I have trouble breathing from here on? The *met*—short for metastasis—was showing so small on the CT scan that only a little tissue would be removed, he said. My breathing would return to normal. The papers I signed releasing him from liability listed many scary outcomes, including bleeding to death.

Dr. Detterbeck pointed to my right side. "We'll do this laparoscopically, with small incisions here."

Just three days before surgery, the doctor's assistant phoned me: the more Dr. Detterbeck thought about my case, he wanted to get his hand inside my chest to feel my right lung for other potential nodules/tumors. He would cut a three-inch incision in the center of my chest just below the rib cage. Would I consent to that?

"Go ahead," I decided fast. My body already had several prominent scars from cancer; what were three more going to matter? The upbeat melanoma patient points to his scars as trophies of battle.

Yale moved swiftly. One week later, I was in the OR. During the four-hour operation, Dr. Detterbeck was amazingly right. While the CT scan found only two nodules, his sensitive surgeon's hand, massaging my lung tissue, felt *two more* nodules. Of the four, two were melanomas, two were benign.

As I awakened in recovery, I was breathing beautifully on my own with no tubes and no pain. So happy, I intentionally drew in heavy, wonderful breaths over and over. "So cool," I mumbled to the recovery nurses as they prepped me to go to a special care room where I would be closely monitored for complications. "Oh wow, this is great!"

Imagine—pieces of my lung had just been removed and I was breathing unassisted.

Turned out to be a remarkably facile surgery. I spent only one night at Yale and was sent home the next night, spending just over 32 hours in the hospital. *From lung surgery!*

Best of all, for the next 12 months my CT scans would show no evidence of cancer.

⁓   ⁓

2009 marked my third year as a cancer patient.

Dr. Kluger gave me hope with her comment that Yale had seen some melanoma patients with no recurrence after lung mets removal. Good oncologists store up these sweet anecdotes of hope. Every three months, the CT and brain scans kept showing clean results. I was flying high and feeling perfect.

Then suddenly came June's scans—almost a year later to the day from when the mets were first seen in my right lung.

"We see two new nodules in your lung again," Harriet broke the news to me.

Another big dip in my cancer journey.

"What about the brain," I asked.

"That's clear," she answered.

"I'm relieved, believe me, that it's not in my brain!", I smiled. Harriet gave me a puzzled look. She had just given her patient bad news, yet I chose to be thrilled that it was *only* in my lung.

I knew the odds. Despite a year of confidence, I prepared myself psychologically for the cancer's return. In the past two years, I had learned that melanoma brain metastases caused the highest mortality, which I feared most of all. There were still several promising treatments ahead. So long as the cancer stayed in my lungs and nowhere else, I convinced myself, I could still beat it.

"Can Dr. Detterbeck operate again?", I asked.

"No, this time the location of the mets would make the surgery more dangerous," Harriet replied.

～～   ～～

Aside from some experimental trials, Yale had just one more FDA-approved treatment for my melanoma: Interleukin-2. It was another substance that would fire up the immune system, just like Interferon, in hopes of triggering a fight-the-invader response.

When my two lung tumors grew to a certain size, Dr. Kluger scheduled me in October 2009 for the tough treatment—so tough that first I had to pass a comprehensive stress test, and be hospitalized for two weeks so doctors could monitor me constantly.

Interleukin, like Interferon, is a substance that's already in your body. It's a type of immune system signaling molecule, instrumental in the body's natural response to infection and in seeing the difference between foreign bodies and self. By administering high doses of IL-2, the Doctors hope the body will recognize the melanoma as a foreign object and fight it.

The published scientific success rates for IL-2 were dismal: partial response of only 15%, and complete elimination of the cancer—only 6% of all patients. But to a stage four melanoma patient with few other options, it's an easy decision. We see hope in those low rates.

Monday afternoon the second week of October, I reported to the 9th floor medical oncology unit for this treatment I dreaded and embraced simultaneously. Yale gave me a private room and quickly put a PICC catheter line in my right arm to infuse the IL-2 and test blood.

"Let the fun begin!", I joked to my nurse as the first bag of IL-2 got hooked up to my *friend*—my IV pole—and began dripping into my veins. Yale wanted me to take as many doses as I could tolerate—like seven or eight in each of the two weeks. There would be one week "off" in between for me to recuperate at home. So essentially it would be a four-week ordeal: two weeks in-hospital, and two weeks to recuperate at home.

By Wednesday, I had the full-blown side-effects: fever and chills, flushing of the face and body, nausea, diarrhea, mental confusion, fast heart beats, aches and pains. My skin erupted in a terrible itchy rash as my immune system turned on my skin. Yale pumped IV fluid into me constantly, so much that I put on over 22 pounds of water-retention weight. The IL-2 causes dangerous drops in blood pressure due to capillary leakage, prompting the nurses to wake you up at least every two hours to measure blood pressure. Plus, they made me measure my urine every time. I didn't want to eat or sleep. By Saturday morning, they wouldn't let me go home until my very low blood pressure reached the right minimum. At home for the interval week, my exhaustion and appetite loss took five days to subside.

And then it was time for me to return for the second week of treatment, where the awful side effects were no less severe—just more known.

Dr. Kluger ordered another round of CT and brain scans in December 2009 to measure IL-2's effect on my cancer.

"No change for the better," she said solemnly when I saw her then. "In fact there might have been some growth."

Yale billed my insurance $285,000 for two weeks of IL-2 treatment. It had no effect.

Harriet and I plotted our next steps. I had exhausted all the FDA-approved regimens. Only experimental treatments remained to save my life.

Together we made a decision to invest our hope and confidence in a promising new science that, failing all else, could save my life—and the lives of thousands others.

All cancer patients go on a memorable journey. It's a long road with twists and turns, potholes, hills, peaks, and valleys. Often you want to forget the unpleasant experiences. Cancer warriors can choose to fear their journey and give in to their primordial fear of the unknown or expectations of the worst. Or, they can embrace the excursion with joy, wonder, and hope. I decided to take the latter route, and was so much better off for the ride.

Research

Ruth Halaban waited patiently outside the Yale operating room for something near and dear to a research scientist: fresh cancerous tumor tissue from surgery. She had done this many times in her 40 years' work researching skin cancer, particularly melanoma.

It was my body inside on the operating table. Dr. Detterbeck carefully retrieved the four suspected melanoma nodules from my right lung. Two of them proved to be cancerous metastases. The tiny nodules, each measuring less than two centimeters, were carefully placed in a special flask and handed over to Dr. Halaban, who ran across the street to her research labs in the sprawling Yale medical complex.

Immediately, with the clock ticking, her team of researchers went to work cultivating my cancer cells in nutritional solutions and Petri dishes.

"Your cells grow very well in the lab," my oncologist, Dr. Harriet Kluger, would tell me repeatedly. I was both happy and horrified at the same time.

"If they grow well in the lab, I guess that means they're growing *too well* inside me," I shot back with a half-smile.

I became a research rat. Nothing in my battle with cancer has given me more pride and hope. And my total, unending commitment to research may have saved my life.

Going into that first appointment with Harriet, I knew beforehand how involved she was in melanoma research.

"You can use me for whatever research or trials you want," I assured Harriet the first time I met her. "It would be an honor, really. What papers can I sign?"

Those turned out to be fateful words that would expose me to an amazing side of cancer that not many people fully understand or appreciate. The statistics are staggering: at least $6 billion is spent just on cancer research every year in the United States, involving tens of thousands of researchers who work in government agencies, universities, hospitals, nonprofit organizations, and private corporations. Every year, 1.6 million Americans are diagnosed with some form of cancer. Close to 600,000 succumb to cancer-related deaths annually. There are 11 million Americans who are cancer survivors—a number growing because of the work of researchers.

The real story of cancer is this massive assault mankind is waging to prevent and treat the disease. A century from now, people will look back with awe at this period of time.

Once I offered myself to research, Yale's medical community ran with it. I mean they *really* went all-out.

Dr. Halaban—whom I affectionately called "Dr. Ruth"—immediately gave my cancer cell line an official name, "YUHEF." The first two letters stood for "Yale University" and the last three were the first letters of my last name. My cells would be used over and over in one experiment after another.

Dr. Ruth and her team of nearly 10 scientists and technicians worked almost entirely on melanoma. They began the intricate process of mapping out my body's genome—the sequence code of my genes. The secret to curing or preventing cancer may lie in genetics.

A native of Israel, Dr. Halaban had degrees in genetics and biology. She dedicated most of her life's work to specializing in melanoma. Her research goals were: 1) to identify novel tumor suppressors and oncogenes that are aberrantly suppressed or expressed in primary and metastatic melanoma compared to normal melanocytes in your skin, 2) to understand the underlying molecular mechanisms that lead to these changes; and 3) identify novel mutations and targets for therapy.

That Yale allowed all of this effort to go forward amazed me. The University's College of Medicine and Yale-New Haven Hospital are cemented together in a unique bond for forging new treatments and medical discoveries. Funding for Dr. Ruth's work came from many sources, the largest of which was a major long-term grant from the National Cancer Institute (NCI), part of the federal National Institutes of Health (NIH). Yale was designated by NIH as one of the nation's comprehensive cancer centers.

Robert V. Heffernan

"We have an opening for a *patient advocate*," Harriet proposed at one of my many appointments with the good doctor. "Would you be interested?"

The Doctor sensed an activist in me, knowing my history of working for the United States Senate and being executive director of three state associations.

The federal NIH/NCI research grant to Yale required the researchers to get real input from *patient advocates*, who would advise the scientists on the directions they took and their sensitivity to patient needs.

"Sure, I'm in!," I answered Harriet. I wanted to involve myself any way I could.

Weeks later, the four Yale melanoma patient advocates, including myself, and each a survivor of the cancer, met over lunch and discussed ways to get more closely connected to the researchers.

That summer, by coincidence, Yale hosted a meeting of the nation's prominent melanoma researchers, and invited me along with the other advocates to sit in on the proceedings. The scientists came from places like M.D. Anderson Cancer Center in Houston, Dana Farber in Boston, Memorial Sloan Kettering in New York City, and University of Pittsburgh, among many others. Their presentations, tailored for scientist-to-scientist, strained my laymen understanding. But those great institutions also sent their patient advocates. The more I talked with other patients and melanoma professionals, the more hope and connections I collected.

"You know I'll be out for a while," fellow patient advocate Mary Russell told me and our other two advocates at a lunch in New Haven. I sat up in my chair to hear more clearly her soft voice.

Like most melanoma and cancer patients, you couldn't tell from looking at her the true extent of her disease. She was the picture of good health, but inside her abdomen there were multiple tumors throughout.

"I'm going to NIH in Bethesda (Maryland) for the TIL treatment," Mary nodded hopefully to us. "I'll probably be there for three or four weeks."

My ears perked up. "What's 'TIL'?", I asked. If a fellow melanoma patient was going for a new treatment I didn't know about, I wanted the scoop. The way my cancer was headed at the time, multiple tumors were a real possibility for me.

Mary Russell would be one of the first Yale patients chosen for this very promising new science at the world's leading medical research facility, the National Institutes of Health (NIH). Researchers there had discovered that the body often makes specialized white cells to fight a cancerous tumor. NIH scientists called them *tumor infiltrating lymphocytes*, or TIL cells. Mary explained the NIH doctors had already removed some of her tumors with the TIL cells attached. The NIH lab was growing her new cells, and then would infuse them back into her body to fight the cancer. Before they did that, NIH would first take down her immune system. It would be a risky and very tough procedure.

Weeks and weeks later after that lunch, no answer came

back from my many e-mails to Mary. She was a very sick woman as she endured the TIL therapy. She contracted a nasty infection during the treatment and was mostly confined to her bed for over four weeks in the NIH complex just outside the nation's capital, Washington D.C.

But she made it through and returned to New Haven to recuperate.

Astonishingly, the tumors in Mary's body slowly disappeared in the months following her TIL treatment. She trekked to Bethesda once a month for CT scans and brain MRIs. Her TIL cells were working.

Six months later, one large melanoma tumor in Mary's abdomen persisted on the scans. That bothered the NIH doctors, especially since all the other tumors had mostly withered away. They convinced Mary—a devoted research supporter like myself—to let them remove that big tumor in yet another surgery.

Inside the NIH operating room, the team of surgeons despaired as they opened her abdomen. They saw the big tumor and removed it easily. But all throughout her stomach area, they saw little black spots—the signature color of melanoma metastases. To the NIH specialists, it was a sad sight.

One by one, with Mary unconscious on the OR table, the surgeons sliced out the black spots. Each time, the NIH lab immediately reported back: "benign", "benign", "benign." They were all dead melanomas. Her new TIL cells had killed the cancer wherever they found it.

Mary waited anxiously 10 more days as the NIH pathologists examined every particle of her large remaining tumor under their powerful microscopes. There was **not** a single live cancer cell in it.

For the next several years, her scans came back clean. Research had taken Mary Russell from the precipice of stage four cancer and near-certain death, to a total remission, and quite possibly a *cure*.

◦~ ~◦

We all hate and avoid *failure*. It's our human nature desiring to *succeed*. But in the history of medicine, failure has sometimes spurred the greatest advances. Melanoma might possibly one day be seen as a shining example of this.

Melanoma was never what I call a *glory cancer*. By that I mean it has few public champions to spur necessary research. Breast cancer affected hundreds of prominent celebrities—such as Betty Ford, Nancy Reagan, Elizabeth Edwards, Melissa Etheridge, Sheryl Crow, and ABC's Robin Roberts, Carly Simon—and thereby inspired an outpouring of massive financial resources for research, the most of all cancers. Look what Lance Armstrong did to raise awareness of testicular cancer. The few prominent sufferers of my cancer would rather you didn't know. Maureen Reagan died of melanoma brain mets in 2001. The 2008 Republican candidate for President, John McCain, showed scars of melanoma surgery on his face, but his campaign didn't want voters to focus on *that*.

Total yearly spending on melanoma research in America is around $150 million, a tiny fraction of the $6 billion spent on all cancer research. Of that, $108 million came out of NIH alone. By not being forefront in the public eye, melanoma has trailed behind in attracting research investments. Melanoma's total research community could fit in a small meeting room.

From the get-go, melanoma lagged far behind in finding effective treatments. But that never deterred the researchers immersed in the disease. Like Ruth Halaban, Harriet Kluger, and several dozen others, they toiled away in their small labs around the world, mostly unknown to the 70,000 melanoma patients in the U.S. They were driven by a silent passion to find answers for a terrible cancer that needed their dedication.

Most all chemotherapy substances had no effect on long-term survival of melanoma patients. Melanoma is one of the few cancers stubbornly resistant to chemo. The failure of chemo spurred the few practicing melanoma researchers to look elsewhere for workable remedies. They chose to zoom in on genetics and the body's immune system. I boldly predict their work may change the course of all cancer care in the future—turning failures into saving lives.

Add to the list of exemplary melanoma researchers: Dr. Steven Rosenberg of NIH. As a young doctor in the Boston area in the late 1960s and early 1970s, he chose to focus on cancer and surgery in an era where cancer was usually a death sentence.

He became intrigued—maybe even obsessed—by those few cancer patients who mysteriously beat back the disease when most others perished. While some attributed these miracles to prayer or good luck, Dr. Rosenberg believed something else was going on inside their bodies. He was betting that a patient's internal immune system could be triggered to attack cancer as if it were unfriendly bacteria or viruses. But how to do it?

Failure of conventional anti-cancer regimens to cure people would instigate this brilliant man to develop the very treatment that wiped out Mary Russell's melanoma. He emerged as a pioneer in developing the first effective immunotherapies for selected patients with advanced cancer.

Dr. Rosenberg became chief of surgery at NIH's National Cancer Institute shortly after leaving Boston, and he stayed there ever since. As the most cited clinician in the world in the field of oncology between 1981 to 1998, he could have worked anywhere he wanted, and he could have retired long ago. Yet nothing could shake his resolve that he was on the right research track—no matter how long it would take. And the world's largest medical research facility—the National Institutes of Health—gave him the freedom and resources to pursue his dream.

Dr. Rosenberg's amazing book, *The Transformed Cell*, tells the story of how he searched for what he termed *killer cells* way back in the early 1980s. Adoptive cell transfer and cloning the TIL cells in the lab were his concepts, first tried on patients at NIH in the early 2000s. Preliminary results showed he was definitely on to something big, but it would take maybe 10 years altogether to refine the techniques to the point that it would become an accepted medical practice—approved by FDA, covered by Medicare and private insurers, and practiced by hospitals worldwide.

Steve Rosenberg is a human monument to determination. The long-running distinguished path of Dr. Rosenberg was about to cross my own melanoma path.

⁓

"We could probably get you into some trials here at Yale," my oncologist offered to me in the exam room of the Yale Cancer Center. "There's an Ipi trial, maybe some others." Dr. Kluger was referring to a promising new human monoclonal antibody *Ipilimumab* developed by Bristol-Myers Squibb that worked by activating the immune system.

Christmas 2009 was only two weeks away. Harriet had just delivered to me the not-unexpected news that four weeks of the tortuous Interleukin-2 treatment on my melanoma had failed. It did nothing for me; my tumors grew. I sat on the exam table wondering if this Christmas might be my last. Who knew what the New Year held for me?

Every possible treatment was experimental from here on.

It's a game of strategy for both doctors and cancer patients. I knew what treatments—licensed and experimental—were out there because I worked hard to investigate them and connect myself. My strategy was to get the cancer before it traveled to my brain.

"I want the TIL. Can you get me in?," I said solemnly, staring directly into the Doctor's eyes. "If I did the other trials, they might disqualify me for TIL, right?"

Harriet nodded yes.

"You'd be a perfect candidate, but we're going to have to work hard to get you in. There are no guarantees they'll accept you.," she cautioned. "Maybe ask Mary or Mario to put in a good word for you?" Dr. Mario Sznol, another astute melanoma specialist at Yale, was one of Dr. Rosenberg's protégés, recruited away from NIH.

I confess: from the first time I learned about Dr.

Rosenberg's wondrous new TIL concept of using my own cells to fight cancer, I sensed I might one day end up there. Something told me all the other treatments and surgeries wouldn't stop my cancer. That day had come. Plus, I personally knew a patient, my friend Mary, who benefitted immensely from TIL. That it would be the most grueling cancer experience didn't concern me. Research had to find cures for melanoma, and I was probably going to die anyway without the TIL procedure.

"Let's do it," I said firmly without hesitation.

"OK, we'll get right to work on the referral," Harriet answered, forcing a smile.

At the time I was trying to pick up on her restrained attitude. I thought she'd be more excited for me. She was worried I might not be admitted into NIH. Also, my decision to go to NIH would remove me from much of her doctoral care and hand my case over largely to the doctors at NIH, 300 miles south of Connecticut. Both of us had been through so much in the past three years, fighting a common enemy. I owed my health and survival to her.

As I stood up in the exam room to leave, Dr. Kluger gave me a hug and a cheek-kiss. I so treasured her personal touch and support.

The Yale staff spent the next two days gathering all my medical records and completing the paperwork required by the National Institutes of Health, then sent it all by FedEx to Bethesda. Thousands of hopeful patients try each year to get into NIH. Thousands are politely rejected because they're not the right candidates for one of the trials. For many, including me, it's often their last hope.

At any given moment, there could be 1,500-2,000 clinical trials going on at the NIH campus in Maryland. To be admitted to one of them, the patient must *precisely* fit the protocol/standards of the experimental trial. For the TIL adoptive cell study, I had to be in good health to withstand the rigors of another surgery to remove a tumor *and* harvest my TIL cells, THEN tolerate my immune system being taken down. How paradoxical is that: an end-stage cancer patient in optimum health? Yet I was strong and healthy.

The TIL protocol demanded a specific leukocyte antigen type. I had to be negative for HIV and hepatitis because my immune system had to be normal going in to the regimen. My hematology, serology, and blood chemistries had to be just so. I couldn't be pregnant or a heavy smoker. My heart had to be in good shape. I couldn't have brain mets. There was a list of other prior treatments that would have disqualified me.

Ironically, I had to have *enough* cancer. NIH needed a good-sized tumor to retrieve the TIL cells from, and then they needed some tumors remaining in my body to measure the treatment's effect. On this score, Harriet warned me I was borderline. Fortunately, my tumors were still tiny, but that could also work against me.

Mary Russell sent an e-mail the next day to Dr. Rosenberg with "Referral of A Friend" in the subject line. Yale's Dr. Sznol offered to call Rosenberg, his former boss, or the key NIH decision makers, but he thought I was such a perfect specimen for the TIL protocol that they would accept me on the face of my medical records without his intervention.

The following Tuesday, less than a week later, my phone rang. An NIH staffer wanted to schedule me to come to Bethesda for an assessment session the following week, Christmas week. Excitement overcame me.

When NIH draws your blood, they take LOTS of blood. Like 10 to 13 tubes of blood. Just about *every* visit. My eyes popped out when I saw the phlebotomist print out all the tube labels.

"It's for research, you know," the phleb joked with me as she poked a butterfly needle into my arm. Blood draw is the routine first stop for most NIH patients.

My Mom rode down to Bethesda, Maryland with me for this critical first visit. We sat in the third floor waiting room of the NIH Clinic, unsure whether the six-hour trip would bear fruit. But we were hopeful. Christmas 2009 was just three days away.

It took a while to find our way into the NIH Clinical Center at the north end of the huge modern campus that fills the equivalent area of 10 city blocks. We went through airport-style security upon entering the visitor gate, complete with metal detectors, luggage x-ray, and auto search. To understand the sheer scale at NIH, about 10% of the agency's *$31 billion* budget supports projects conducted by nearly 6,000 scientists in its own laboratories, most of whom work on the Bethesda campus—its funding made possible by you, the taxpayer, through your federal taxes. NIH has its own police force, and its own fire department, and even its own subway stop.

I smiled when I saw the official name on the multi-floored, multi-winged building: *Mark O. Hatfield Clinical Research Center.* The nation's largest hospital devoted entirely to medical research was named after a Republican U.S. Senator from Oregon who served in office when I worked for the U.S. Senate in the late 1970s.

Since NIH opened in 1953, more than 400,000 clinical research participants like myself had come in search of medical cures, bringing their unselfish desire to help others by contributing to science. NIH engenders pride from every American, making ground-breaking discoveries weekly, employing the nation's brightest scientific experts, and giving 50,000 competitive grants to more than 325,000 researchers at over 3,000 universities, medical schools, and other research institutions in every state and around the world.

If NIH accepted me into their TIL research, I would be leaving one class act—Yale—for the mother ship of medical science, NIH.

After a long wait, a social worker called my name. In a small conference room, the woman gave me a standard briefing on what I could expect *if I became an NIH patient.*

There would be no charge for my medical care under the specific protocol I was brought in for, the NIH social worker explained. NIH would pay for everything. There would be no reason to contact my insurance company, no deductible, no claims forms. Once the treatment was finished, NIH would transfer me back to my at-home doctors. If I developed an illness not related to the research protocol, it would have to be handled back at home.

NIH would even pay for my travel to and from Bethesda. They'd also help me pay for my hotel room with a small $50-a-night stipend. (Bethesda area hotel rates were triple that.)

And like my at-home hospitals and doctors, NIH required I sign a long, detailed release of liability form. After all, this was experimental treatment with a higher degree of risk.

I would be assigned a social worker to help navigate the NIH process. And, best of all, an elegant hotel had been built on the campus a few years earlier where family members could stay free of charge for longer-term admissions.

NIH treated its patients royally, to say the least.

30 minutes later, two doctors and a research nurse met with me in a cramped exam room—each one part of Dr. Rosenberg's team. They had reviewed all my Yale records and wanted to be sure I fully understood what the TIL treatment entailed. I suspect they were also checking out my mental outlook and enthusiasm.

"There could be one problem," Dr. Jenny Hong said. "Your largest tumor is located between your esophagus and your right lung in a position where frankly we don't see how the surgeon could get it. Maybe he'll see it differently," she shrugged.

Hong said she would let me know the decision of the NIH thoracic surgeon, probably after the first of the New Year.

Mom and I drove home not knowing what would

happen. My foot was halfway in the NIH door. I spent a worrisome Christmas at her home in Vermont, dubious about my prospects for the New Year 2010.

"Mr. Heffernan, the surgeon thinks he can remove your tumor with no problems," Dr. Hong said cheerfully when she phoned the first week of January 2010. "When can we schedule you?"

"That means I'm in?"

"You're in for the TIL procedure, yes," Dr. Hong confirmed.

Imagine being elated about a dangerous surgery followed by potentially treacherous experimental medical treatment. Everything in life is relative. I felt myself levitate off my office chair with sheer joy of qualifying for a process that could save my life, or put me through hell, or both.

I set the date for the third Tuesday in January.

Dr. King Kwong (his real name!) asked me to take off my shirt in my room at the NIH hospital. I had arrived in Bethesda that Tuesday afternoon and would be in surgery the very next morning.

An expert thoracic surgeon, Dr. Kwong used his finger to draw a long imaginary curved line on my back, from the top around my right scapula (shoulder blade). "We'll make the incision here and retrieve your tumor from your back side."

Moments later, an anesthesiologist arrived to explain she

would implant an epidural line to pump a potent anesthetic into my back that would stay with me for the next few days. Translation: this would be a *painful* procedure.

Not long after, a research nurse asked me to sign a living will and a 12-page document disclosing the many dangers of the whole TIL process. Didn't matter what it said; I was going to sign it. The paper listed scary conditions previous TIL patients had experienced: loss of sight, severe infections, paralysis, respiratory distress, severe nausea, yada, yada, and the possibility of *death*. All of this, I chose to risk in the name of research, and the sheer desire to *live*.

Inside the NIH surgical suite the next morning, Dr. Kwong pulled out a 3.6 centimeter tumor that once was a lymph node the cancer had taken over—outside my right lung up against my esophagus. I spent the next 24 hours in intensive care.

Outside the operating room, Dr. Mark Dudley and his team took my tumor to their unique lab facility close by on the same floor to begin the process of parsing out my TIL cells and growing them to a high number—their target count was *50 billion* cells. A native of Connecticut with degrees in biology from MIT and Stanford, Mark was a treasured lieutenant in Dr. Rosenberg's team, developing wild new techniques for not only reproducing those anti-cancer cells on a large-scale, but also tinkering with genetic fixes that would make them more powerful once transplanted back into a person's body.

The best thing about the whole TIL concept is the engineered cells are *my own cells*, not donor cells like the kind used in a bone marrow transplant. So there are no rejection issues.

Monday morning, five days after my surgery, I felt some of the strongest pain ever in my life. I appealed to Mark Dudley to visit his lab and maybe see my new TIL cells. He invited me inside his wondrous laboratory, pulled out a dish with a liquid containing nutrients and Interleukin-2. That same substance which made me so sick at Yale for four weeks back in October helps grow TIL cells. Turns out, the little buggers just *love* it.

"Here, take a look in this microscope," Mark motioned as he fine-tuned the focus dial.

Inside the lens, clear as could be, I could see remnants of my cancer cells with these very active, busy, whitish cells wiggling and pushing hard against the melanoma.

"Oh my God, those are my TIL cells?," I asked him.

Mark Dudley grinned broadly and shook his head.

Tears gushed out my eyes and down my cheeks. I wrapped my arms around Mark and gave him the warmest hug.

Those beautiful TIL cells were my last hope for living.

One hurdle after another stood between me and the TIL treatment. Each alone would have stopped the process.

The first barrier for many patients is enduring the surgery to find if the TIL cells are there or not. Hurdle number two is inducing enough cells to grow in the lab past that magic 50 billion figure. Assuming the patient can leap past other barriers—surviving the depletion of your immune system, infection, etc.—then there's the unpredictability of whether the new TIL cells overcome the cancer and reproduce to continue fighting within the body.

Research of the NIH teams would answer these and hundreds of other questions, but this detailed work takes years.

A major scientific report published a few months earlier co-authored by Dr. Rosenberg and Dr. Dudley said, "Adoptive cell therapy is the best available treatment for

patients with metastatic melanoma. In a recent series of three consecutive clinical trials using increasing lymphodepletion, before infusion of autologous tumor infiltrating lymphocytes (TIL), objective response rates between 49% and 72% were seen."

No other treatment for melanoma came anywhere close to these success rates. In a lecture at Yale months following my treatment, Dr. Rosenberg said NIH was seeing long-term, durable remissions in as many as 30% of the TIL patients. As time wore on, that figure could rise as more TIL patients were tested. He came so close to calling it a cure for some patients, but more time was needed.

Recuperating at home for the next three weeks, pain from my back surgery persisted. It bothered me so much I made an appointment to see Harriet at Yale, where she chided me for not being patient enough. "You had a *major* surgery, you know," she admonished me.

Before NIH would bring me back to Bethesda, I had to wait anxiously in Connecticut for word from the NIH lab that my cells had multiplied to that magic number: 50 billion.

In the meantime, NIH ordered my overnight return to Bethesda for something called *Leukapheresis*. Flat on my back for five hours, blood ran out one arm into a machine and back into my body in the other arm, collecting large numbers of white blood cells. Dr. Dudley's lab would insert my TIL cells into the white cells using an inactivated (harmless) virus in a process called retroviral transduction.

Another hurdle I jumped over handily.

⌇⌇

"Your cells are almost ready!," Dr. Hong called from NIH February 15.

"Wow, so they're growing well?," I asked.

Dr. Hong said if I came down to NIH the next week, there would be enough TIL cells to start the treatment. We set the admission date for February 24, 2010.

Nervous, ecstatic, and anxious, I spent the next week frantically getting my life ready to be out of commission for as long as the TIL process would take—at least three full weeks in the NIH hospital, possibly four, followed by longer rest at home. My husband Allen got time off to be with me through the family and medical leave law. Mom would drive down from Vermont for the whole time. The beautiful Safra Lodge, next to the NIH Clinical Center in Bethesda, had a room waiting to house them for the entire treatment period—*for free.*

NIH's bedside TVs doubled as computers, so I could log in to my office computer 300 miles away, and keep working as if I was there. For the first time in 20 years, I would not be in Connecticut to manage one of my large trade shows. Leaders of the three state associations I directed pitched in to help me out, supporting me all the way.

Working night and day, I got as much done as I could, compressing five weeks of duties into six days. Finally leaving my Connecticut office the morning of February 24, I could hear my secretary Jackie sniffling tears as I walked down the hallway. Everyone in my life knew the enormous risk ahead of me.

NIH nurse Sandra Cooper, a veteran of NIH's oncology third floor, walked in my room dressed like she was handling a hazmat substance. Indeed she was. Wearing goggles, a mask, and a yellow gown, Sandy's gloved hands attached a plastic bag full of Cytoxan to my IV pole. She connected the tube to the Hickman port in my upper right chest that would feed all my treatment into lines leading directly to a major heart artery.

"Ready?," her beautiful Jamaican-born face smiled.

"I'm here for the cure. Let's go!," I flashed back two thumbs up.

Cytoxan was so powerful there were special rules for how medical staff handled it. Yet they were putting it directly into my veins. The drug would instantly start killing the white cells making up my immune system.

Drip, drip, drip. Seemed like only 30 minutes had passed, and the Cytoxan flowed into my body. I turned to my Mom sitting beside my NIH bed, "What am I doing to my beautiful immune system?" They were second thoughts, but my resolve was firm. I lay there hoping the next three weeks would not bring any infections.

It seemed so counterintuitive: destroying the immune system but using it simultaneously. Dr. Rosenberg's team had discovered the TIL cells—specialized little soldiers of the body's vast immune system—worked best when they had the body to themselves. All the other white cells—their "cousins"— act as bullies, getting in the way of the TIL cells trying to attack cancer. By taking down the bulk of my immune system with powerful chemo drugs, it was like removing all the traffic off the Interstate highways and giving the TIL cells exclusive open roads to go anywhere inside the body, in search of the cancer they had evolved to fight, without interference or logjams.

Just two hours later, I ran to the sink and vomited. So began three weeks of the worst nausea I ever experienced— uninterrupted, night and day.

The next day, Allen borrowed the set of barber clippers stored on the NIH oncology floor and shaved off all my head hair. I knew I was destined to loose it anyhow for months.

It would take a full week for two chemos—Cytoxan and Fludarabine—to take down my immune system close to zero.

～ ～

"You're neutropenic, let's go!", NIH nurse Sandy hollered at me the following Thursday morning, almost a week later, as I watched TV in the lounge at the end of the hallway. Lab results confirmed I was officially minus a working immune system. Sandy ordered me back to my now-private room stat, where she would begin administering heavy-hitting drugs to protect me from literally dozens of potential opportunistic infections—anti-virals, antibiotics, anti-fungals.

But now, without an immune system, I was ready to receive my new TIL cells. I would have to wear a mask and wash my hands repeatedly. Warning signs to visitors were posted on the door to my room. All medical personnel had to be gowned and gloved to enter.

I felt like crap. Nausea overpowered me so much that at one point the doctors had me on five different anti-puke medications plus wrist pressure bands used for motion sickness. The drugs hardly cut that draining, exhausting feeling. Still, I forced myself to eat something constantly—smaller portions of food more often. NIH's dieticians created a biocare slush, sort of like a crushed-ice Slush Puppy, loaded with nutrients that melted in your mouth and slithered down to a revolting stomach. The only true nausea relief came with sleep.

I shed nearly 30 pounds from the rigors of the TIL procedure, definitely a nicer side effect, although I wouldn't recommend it as weight loss therapy.

I chose to endure nausea and exhaustion as my trophy, the small price I had to pay for the chance at a new cure, and my contribution to research. Whenever the pangs of sickness overwhelmed me, I forced my mind to focus on the big goal. Desktop work on my bedside computer plus the love of my ever-present Mom and partner helped take my mind off myself. Those diversions help many cancer patients persevere.

Friday, March 5, 2010. One of those beautiful, emotional, unforgettable days that stays with you forever.

We waited impatiently for my TIL cells to arrive from the NIH lab. My body was ready.

TIL lab director Dr. Mark Dudley and his crew had been working hard growing and prepping the cells up to the last moment. The walk from his lab to my room was less than five minutes away.

"Here they are—67.2 billion of them," nurse Sandy boasted with a smile as she rushed into my room at 10:05am. In her hands, a simple clear plastic bag measured about ten inches wide by ten inches tall.

"That's it, all 67 billion of them...in that little bag?," I asked in astonishment. Dr. Dudley really knew how to grow these cells, blowing 17 billion more past the research protocol's minimum requirement for 50 billion cells.

The cells started flowing from the IV pole through the IV tubing and into my chest catheter. Sandy stood there the whole time, massaging the bag with her warm gloved hands. The TIL cells have the habit of clumping in the IV fluid, and a bigger, thicker tube carried them into my body.

"Go, go go!," I cheered the cells on, as my nurse smiled her approval. "Get that cancer!" I felt paternalistic towards those cells, like they were my *kids*. They were all mine, born outside my body but made entirely of my DNA. They were coming inside me to save me, to kill the very enemy of life, cancer.

I looked over at my Mom, quietly crying in the corner of my room. Allen got all choked up. This was the moment of a four-year battle, the climax of years of research and hope.

I savored every moment of the infusion—it took just 36 minutes for all 67.2 billion cells to surge through my veins.

The growing pains I suffered as a child came back the next week. Once the new TIL cells were inside my body, the NIH doctors had to rebuild my immune system as quickly as they could. Nurses started injecting me with Neupogen, a drug stimulating the bone marrow to increase production of neutrophils, those essential white cells forming the bulk of the immune system. My bones began to ache and ache, just like growing pains. It was actually a good sign.

"We can send you home if you have no infection and your white cell counts reach 5,000," Dr. Hong told me.

Over the next 10 days, my counts recovered slowly, then it seemed my immune system roared back to life. The Friday a week after getting my new cells, the white cell count was 50. Saturday it was 200. Sunday it zoomed to 1,500. NIH let me out on a special pass that afternoon to spend the day and evening with Mom and Allen at NIH's Safra Lodge—first time out of the hospital in three weeks. I felt good enough to leave the NIH campus with Allen on a trip to the grocery store, but once inside the store felt so weak I wondered if I could walk back to the car. Still, it felt great to sleep in a real bed at Safra.

Monday morning, the NIH lab reported an astonishing 8,000 white cell count.

"Would you like to go home?," a smiling Dr. Hong teased me upon learning the labs.

"Oh, please, can I?", I gushed as my eyes welled up with tears. I rushed over and gave the doctor a big bear hug.

Per usual, the discharge process seemed like it took forever. A nurse sternly commanded me to wear two medical alert bracelets: "NO STERIODS UNLESS MEDICAL EMERGENCY" and "GIVE IRRADIATED BLOOD PRODUCTS ONLY." Those inscribed orders signaled to other medical types that I had a living treatment ongoing inside my body, which could not be jeopardized in any way.

Riding up Interstate 95 back to Connecticut, the car was overloaded with three weeks of luggage and supplies, barely room enough for Allen (driving), myself, and Mom. I was weak and hairless, but thrilled to be going home.

The cure for cancer may not come with a profit motive.

Indeed, that's why the nation's war on cancer always had bipartisan support from all political parties. Americans could not rely solely on pharmaceutical companies to find cures and treatments. The value of NIH to the American people is its independence from the pressures of profit to go after any and all leads in finding novel solutions to disease and suffering.

Those 67.2 billion TIL cells now coursing through my veins were a prime example. Adoptive cell therapy could not have been developed by Pfizer, or Bristol Myers, or Astra Zeneca, because it wasn't a patentable pill you took. Yet, the whole concept of finding target fighter cells specific to one cancer is something only independent researchers like those at NIH had the freedom and time to pursue. And their grants enable similar pursuits at places like Yale all across the country.

NIH's $31 billion annual budget is one of the best investments of our tax dollars. If you want to put a face on this, look at me.

Suffering a serious disease like cancer, I strongly felt a moral duty to offer myself up to research. So long as cures are elusive, I wanted to help as much as I could.

The treatments we have today are available because millions of people over hundreds of years participated in advance of us. They did this for us. It was their moral imperative to leave this legacy to humankind.

Think about it: everything medical comes out of research, from the adhesive bandage we put on a cut in our skin to the simple aspirin to the most complicated organ transplant. All of it had to be researched in one form or another. More than anything else, research is the very foundation of all medicine.

At many research institutions like Yale-New Haven and the National Institutes of Health, body tissues and fluids will be used for research whether the patient knows or not. Their consent is implicit in their choice to be treated there. That's exactly as it should be, I felt. If this really bothers a patient, they can go to another facility that doesn't engage in research.

I am a part of medical history. My cancer cells are guiding researchers at Yale, NIH, and elsewhere towards a cure. My TIL therapy may one day be the way many cancer patients are treated.

Whether cancer takes my life in the end is irrelevant. I am a research subject of the highest order, and that will always be one of my proudest and most honorable legacies that I will leave to the people of this planet.

Treatment

My jaw dropped open at the sight. As they wheeled me in to the Yale operating room for my first lung surgery, I quickly counted twelve professionals garbed in OR surgical gowns, hats, and masks. So much high-tech equipment filled the room they had trouble maneuvering my gurney into its berth under the arms of giant spotlights hanging from the ceiling.

That was July 2008, year two of cancer for me. Two previous major surgeries to excise the cancer and one full year on Interferon failed to eliminate all stray melanoma cells. The cancer popped up in my right lung.

I had asked Dr. Frank Detterbeck, one of the nation's great thoracic surgeons, if he could hold off giving me general anesthesia until I had a chance to personally thank every person inside the operating room. Probably most surgeons would rather the patient arrive in the OR already unconscious and ready for surgery. But I placed such a high priority on personally connecting with *all* the medical professionals who were trying to save my life. Most patients get to talk with perhaps only one or two attendants who were inside the OR during their surgery—usually the surgeon or anesthesiologist before and after the surgery. The rest you never know about. They go unrecognized. Yet they do sterling work in support of human life.

No doubt several of the OR staffers were Yale medical students. I insisted with each of my doctors that students be part of all my procedures. I felt such a sense of honor and contribution to the advancement of medicine to ask their involvement in my treatment. While some patients fear the inexperience of the in-training medical student, I sought them out with pride. Working on real live cases such as my own, they could become great physicians who would go on to treat thousands more people in the future.

Outside the OR just before I went in, a young female medical student asked, with her Yale professor, if she could insert the first pre-surgical IVs into my arm. "Of course you can," I smiled lying on my back on the gurney, with a surgical cap on my head. She was so nervous. She tried twice and missed both veins. Both attempts made me sore, because they were using a larger-gauge needle for the volume of fluids required for this major surgery. Her professor took over and aced it on the first try. The student felt so bad; I could read it in her face. I touched her arm reassuringly, "Don't worry about it. You're going to become a really good doctor in a few years. Stick with it!"

Inside the OR, with the sea of medical-green gowns, it was hard to tell who was who. When everybody has the same cloaking, they all look alike. But each person had a critical role to play, and were busy working. In a glass-walled small room off to the side, I could see Dr. Detterbeck and some assistants (some students also) looking one last time at the scans of my chest. Nurses and anesthesiologists hooked me up to one machine after another. Both of my arms were outstretched on long boards, where IVs were connected.

"Are you ready, Mr. Heffernan?," asked the good Doctor, finally standing by my side.

"Let me thank everyone," I replied. He motioned for all to stop a moment and look my way. Raising my head off the gurney, I started to talk in a breaking emotional voice.

"Thank you, thank you EVERYONE, for being here today. You're all so important. You all do such wonderful work. I just know that you all are going to give me a long life. I want each of you to know how grateful I am."

I could see their faces smiling, even with masks on. Several shook their heads. The nurses nodded. I heard a chorus of responses, everything from "It's our job," to "So happy to help you, Mr. Heffernan."

"So, let's begin," Dr. Detterbeck said to the team. With that, the anesthesiologist put his special mask to my lips and nose. "Breathe deeply," he said. And out I went.

Their remarkable work that morning gave me another full year of clean scans. Hopefully, each and every one of them went home proud of their roles in serving humanity, alleviating suffering, and curing disease. On this planet, there is no higher service to humankind.

I *chose* to have that surgery on my lung. I *chose* to have the previous two surgeries. I chose to go through a year of Interferon injections, despite the poor success rates. I chose two weeks of inpatient treatment with Interleukin-2. Months later, I would *choose* to have the fourth surgery to harvest TIL cells from yet another tumor, and go through the TIL adoptive cell treatment.

Choice can be a beautiful thing for cancer patients. For the most part, we are in total control of our treatment. We can often control our destiny with the disease.

Sure, doctors recommend this course or that treatment. Sometimes they say no more can be done and urge treatment stop, but even then we can choose to do more, to go somewhere else. Usually, the cancer patient has so many choices.

It's a big world out there for treatment of cancer. Thousands of institutions. Hundreds of thousands of doctors. Virtually every cancer presents many treatment options for patients.

Making choices is so empowering for the patient. That feeling alone is therapeutic. I've told many oncologists and surgeons over the past five years that only when a cancer patient truly feels in control of his/her treatment, can true healing occur. I've advised many patients how important it is that they feel total *confidence* in their treatment. If you don't feel it, do something about it fast, I urge them. Look for other options, other professionals. Time matters with cancer.

I love my local, community hospital just five miles down the road from my home in New Milford, Connecticut, where they have a wonderful regional cancer center. With all due respect to the good doctors there, if I had chosen that lovely institution to handle my melanoma I might not be alive today. Instead, I did my homework and chose to land in Yale-New Haven Hospital over 75 minutes further to the south. It also helped I had a dermatologist who knew the right place for my treatment and steered me there.

Some boutique cancers, such as melanoma, require a precise body of knowledge that resides in only a handful of medical institutions across the U.S. and Canada. I can name on the fingers of my two hands those places where a melanoma patient should go, with Yale being one of them. If I were a woman with breast cancer, my local community hospital would be an excellent choice and could easily handle the treatment regimen. Where we choose to be treated for cancer can sometimes be more critical in leading to a successful outcome than the treatment itself. A particular doctor's or hospital's connection to the world of research in your cancer similarly may lead to the latest treatment others may not even be aware of yet. Indeed, many cancer doctors in small communities excel at their work when they reach out for guidance from experts, and when they share their own successes.

An outstanding medical center is one that knows its own limits; great doctors similarly know theirs. I would hope that my local hospital, if I had gone there, would have the good sense to ship me to another institution that really did have the expertise. But over the years, as I've talked with other patients, I've heard too many bad stories of hospitals and practices that decided they could handle the cancer on their own, despite it being way out of their element of expertise.

Yale-New Haven passed this test of greatness by sending me to the National Institutes of Heath. "You know you're in big trouble when Yale sends you someplace else," I often joked to others. Because of its profound expertise and resources, including one of the world's premier medical schools, Yale is a top destination for treatment. Yet even the Yale melanoma team knew they had gone about as far as they could at that time (late 2009) before offering to refer me to NIH.

And, I *chose* to leave the greatness of Yale for NIH. I just had an intuition that my choices were going to help me whip this cancer. I had that necessary confidence.

In my own family, I witnessed first-hand how choice matters in cancer treatment.

A dear friend of the family, Karen, suddenly developed a brain tumor. She was young, in her 50s, with two children and grandchildren. She chose to be treated at her nearby hospital in a beautiful northwest Connecticut town.

Doctors soon told her the tumor was inoperable. "It's not curable, it's treatable," they told the family. Over the following months, she would endure several debilitating treatments in an effort to beat down the cancer, and buy her precious time on this Earth.

Karen wanted to live so badly. We all felt that for her, with her. She had so much to live for. We watched in sadness as she suffered in her final months, the treatments making her so sick. She chose to put up a fight to the very end, as so many cancer patients do.

My Aunt Charlotte started vomiting for no reason in June 1980, until doctors in Burlington, Vermont diagnosed her with terminal liver cancer. At the time, most liver cancer was a death sentence. In her late 30s with five children, she fought back over the summer, choosing some experimental treatments, desperate to cling to life and be there for her kids.

Charlotte was so sick to the end. Doctors gave her just three-to-five months. She died Labor Day weekend. We were all devastated at the loss.

Another Great Aunt, Ida, was a heavy smoker all her life. In her late 70s, she had lung cancer. Interestingly, she chose *not* to know the details. Both Aunt Ida and my grandmother (her sister) adhered to an age-old backcountry Vermont wisdom: What you don't know won't hurt you. I actually once heard my grandmother say, "They used to tell me don't listen to those doctors, they only tell you bad news."

I laugh every time I lovingly remember both of them; how their mindsets go counter to everything we follow today. Their generation didn't have the mountains of medical information we take for granted today. It was a big deal to even go see a doctor in the first half of 20th century Vermont.

But I can never forget how Aunt Ida handled her last days with lung cancer. She took no anti-cancer drugs or chemotherapy. No radiation. Towards the end, doctors put her on an oxygen tank, which she willingly accepted so she could breathe well and medicine to comfort her. What amazed me was this: Aunt Ida had a fairly good quality end of life. We saw her suffer relatively little. Only her last week or so was tough on her. She chose to forgo aggressive cancer treatment. She chose to put it out of her mind. It's one of those treatment options every cancer patient has.

When you serve on a Board of Directors, the laws of all 50 states require you to follow the duty of care, and the duty of loyalty. I think the same duties might apply to cancer patients in a moral sense, one stronger than any law.

The duty of care requires you to use your best personal skills and judgment in making decisions. For people with cancer, deciding where to go for treatment, which doctor to choose, and what course of treatment ranks among the most important decisions of our life.

I felt a solemn duty to *myself*, to my own body, to find the best possible care and immerse myself in whatever knowledge is available about my cancer.

I believed that I had to take responsibility for my treatment—not lay the entire burden on my medical team. My Uncle Bob, who died of metastatic throat cancer in the 1990s, was a classic example of a patient who did none of this. "What are THEY gonna do to help *me*," I heard him utter about his doctors at the VA Medical Center in Boston, a team who did a good job of keeping him alive for 10 years after diagnosis. Mind you, my dear Uncle said this while smoking cigarettes and drinking beer. In his mind, like many cancer patients, the cancer was *their* problem to deal with, not *his*.

To be fair, not every person has the drive or skill to bone up on facts and latest scientific findings. For some patients, they might fare better if it all was laid on their doctor. Uncle Bob fell in this category.

Today, many cancer patients do their own research, and discover a working knowledge about their affliction. One Internet line alone is sufficient to give us heaps of information about our cancer. We can learn about clinical trials that our own doctor may not yet be aware of. One of the best web sites for this is the NIH-sponsored clinicaltrials.gov, an official portal that pulls together thousands of ongoing experiments for every cancer.

Today's doctors are accustomed to working with the informed patient. Indeed, the optimum relationship between doctor and patient occurs when each knows fully what they're dealing with, and the goals both want to achieve: either a cure or a longer happy life of manageable disease.

I wanted to be careful not to go overboard. Patients who smother their medical teams in data or adopt the I-know-it-all attitude risk turning off their doctors. I've seen it happen. We're working partners in a battle extraordinaire.

But it's *our* body, and *our* life, and *our* future. I embraced my personal duty of care.

A cancer patient's duty of loyalty can be just as important—first to my medical team, and second to the ones I love. Once we patients have gained confidence in selecting the right place, team, and treatment, we need to express great loyalty to those engaged in the battle with us, I believe.

When our doctors and medical team sense a solid loyalty from us, the patients, they'll go to the ends of the earth for us. They'll do much more than the minimum required in the doctor-patient relationship. All human beings have abilities to work harder and deeper beyond what's expected of us, and the world of medicine is no different. Doctors especially appreciate patient commitment to their own wisdom and judgment.

Loyalty builds trust with our doctors to the point that

frank assessments on our condition become imperative and valuable.

More than anything, a cancer patient and his family need both love and loyalty to deal with it all. I know it's asking a lot of a cancer patient to maintain loyalty to his/her loved ones when just enduring the malady takes herculean strength. But I think it's an essential component of treatment.

Today's cancer treatment may be seen 100 years from now as barbaric. For the past century, we could sum it up in three categories: cut it out, radiate it out, or drug it out.

We Yale melanoma patients used to joke that a public education campaign about our cancer would have the slogan, "Got Scars?" You should see scars on my body from four major surgeries, ports, thoroscopic incisions, etc. The first line of treatment for melanoma is almost always "cut it out." Same goes for many cancers today: surgery first. Hundreds of thousands of patients never see another recurrence beyond that. Bravo!

Radiation to kill cancer tumors gained prominence after a Chicago doctor first used it in 1896. Early radiation techniques harmed healthy tissues sometimes more than the cancer itself. The medical world won't give up radiation as a tool against cancer. Instead, they've worked on perfecting the technology. I used to think melanoma brain metastases were deadly until my good friends, fellow Yale patients Mark Driggs and Sam Rich, had gamma knife radiation treatments that pinpointed precise x-rays to zap their tiny tumors deep inside their skulls. They're doing fine at the moment.

Personally, I'm not a fan of chemotherapy—the *drug it out* portion of cancer treatment. The whole concept bothers me from the get-go: infuse a substance that's supposed to kill cancer cells, but often harms other vital bodily functions and makes the patient so sick it hinders quality of life. But it's a staple of modern cancer treatment. No self-respecting oncologist would ever work without chemotherapy as an option.

Lucky for me, since melanoma rarely responds to chemo, I never had it until NIH used Cytoxan, but that was to take down my immune system, not kill the cancer. Pharmaceutical companies have poured much of their research and development energy into finding newer and better chemotherapy drugs, mainly because the return on investment can be high. Chemo is getting better with fewer side effects. We're also learning that chemo may work in ways scientists never thought: sometimes the drugs weaken/change cancer cells enough that the patient's immune system suddenly recognizes them as invaders and attacks them—kind of like the vaccines that uses weakened viruses to stimulate immunity. On the flip side, the chemo may also be killing the very white cells needed to pull this off. This fairly recent finding helps explain why some patients go into remission following chemotherapy.

One unspoken effect of some cancer treatments is that they unwittingly may cause another cancer in the process of curing an existing one. Even today, news stories appear regularly warning that radiation from CT scans may cause cancer elsewhere in the body later on. But scans are too valuable to abandon. Another good friend of mine, Vince Barker, successfully beat back a rare event: breast cancer in men. But three years later he was fighting leukemia, possibly instigated by the treatments for his breast cancer. NIH warned me some of the drugs used in my TIL procedure might cause lymphoma "or other cancers".

The most recent two decades have opened up an exciting fourth genre of cancer treatment: the sciences of genetics and of immunology. Yale has mapped my genome, looking for clues that could give way to new melanoma treatments. They've identified which genes "turn on" melanoma cells and others that work against immune cells fighting them. Once they're armed with this information, the scientists can research targeted drugs. Hospitals like Yale-New Haven now have *genetic counseling*, a novel high-tech approach that analyzes trends in your family heritage and may guide how your cancer is treated.

Advances in immunology, of course, may have saved my own life. Harnessing the power of the body's immune system to fight disease is not new. Jonas Salk's polio vaccine attacked that disease this way and ended it entirely. The TIL adoptive cell therapy that NIH used on my melanoma could potentially become the ground-breaking recipe for curing all cancer—who knows? The NIH doctors targeted immune cells my body had already made to fight the cancer, and super-charged them to go all the way. Three years following that treatment, I'm alive and well, living a normal, healthy life.

Setting aside the barbarism analogy, in fact modern treatments for cancer are saving lives like never before. The war on cancer is a work in progress—a long, painstaking road to finding new remedies that help people beat odds and survive. New therapies come often before the Food and Drug Administration for approval. Countless trials may well produce more. That is a beautiful gift to us cancer survivors.

⁂

We donned on hard hats for a precious honor: the first patients to tour the still-under-construction new Smilow Cancer Hospital attached to Yale-New Haven Hospital. I beamed from ear to ear as we inched our way through unfinished hallways, dodging construction workers.

"We" were the first patient-family advisory council for the new hospital. I eagerly jumped on the appointment and the chance to serve when Yale asked me. The new Council gave a select few cancer survivors a direct line to make input on how Yale delivered treatment, and how patients and families were catered to in the process.

Rising some 14 stories in the New Haven skyline and costing more than half a billion dollars, the new hospital would become a beautiful monument to the treatment of cancer. It would have 168 private rooms for in-hospital cancer patients, plus its own operating rooms, the latest, most sensitive scanning equipment, a cancer-oriented boutique shop, plentiful clinic centers, a rooftop garden, plus fine conference facilities.

As our group moved cautiously around construction supplies, I purposely stayed back for a few solemn, solitary moments staring at the walls of future clinic examination rooms. Their walls were spanking new and clean. Silent. Awaiting the day when patients would enter, full of anxiety.

Looking intently at the walls, I flashed back to my countless clinic appointments where time stood still and thick as my mind raced, worrying *what if* the Doctor delivered this bad news, or that good news.

Most cancer patients get their results and treatment decisions in small exam rooms like these. As you wait on top of the uncomfortable exam table with its phony sanitary paper, it seems like forever before the doctor walks in. The tension in that wait can be unbearable. Once at NIH in Bethesda, a doctor broke away from other appointments and rushed into my room. "I can't stand to watch you pace back-and-forth—your scans are good!," he assured me. "So relax."

I gazed down at the floor where the new hospital hallway and exam room met—a line of fate. A patient could walk across that invisible line feeling absolutely *perfect*, yet unaware of how his/her life could change in an instant after the doctor walks across that same line, shuts the door, and utters, "Here's what we found in your labs (or scans)….". They see things way before a cancer patient would ever feel them. That's what makes hospital and physician exam rooms so momentous. Like rooms of world history where great wars were negotiated to an end, the exam rooms of cancer treatment record personal battles over and over. If exam room walls could talk…..

Those clean walls of Smilow's new clinic exam rooms started fresh. What amazing, heartbreaking, and joyful stories they would amass in the years ahead.

The Smilow Cancer Hospital at Yale would open its doors October 2009, advancing cancer treatment for southern New England.

My cancer has never made me sick. My treatments surely have sickened me. My surgeries caused lots of pain and suffering.

The only time I actually *felt* my cancer was that little bump atop my scalp at the start of it all. Even then, it didn't hurt. Many cancer patients—certainly not all—do not suffer unless a tumor is affecting a nerve (causing pain) or impinges on an internal bodily function.

One of my melanoma buddies had multiple tumors throughout the abdomen, but never knew they were there until a scan for another complaint caught the surprise. Mark Driggs had a melanoma tumor the size of a baseball on his liver, but never felt it.

Cancer often does not make us sick until the latter stages of the disease. Why? Because the cancer cells are accepted by the rest of the body as if they belong there. After all, cancer cells are your own cells. They're not foreign objects in the sense that a virus or alien bacteria might signal *invasion* to the body's immune system. Cancer rarely causes a fever that might alert a person that something is wrong. Normally, it's a lump or a feeling something's not right that leads to a cancer diagnosis. It's a small consolation that this disease can initially spare suffering at the same time it portends great harm and danger.

The research to find *biomarkers* in the blood is a wonderful direction, because doctors can get clues that a cancer might be present way before it's felt any other way.

The paradox of cancer treatment is that it can both save your life and make you sick at the same time. So many patients don't know which to fear more: the treatment or the cancer. We place such a high priority on life and survival that we can accept treatment side effects as simply part of the task of staying alive. In this day and age, we understand that it goes with the territory of being a cancer patient.

A Vermont woman whom I considered a "second mother", Phyllis, knew the risks of her treatment for advanced breast cancer. Doctors told her the chemo prescribed for her was the only way to manage the disease and lengthen her life. She didn't die of the cancer itself. The chemo so weakened her immune system that she died of a massive infection. But she chose to stay on this planet for years more than if she had not taken any treatment at all. Her last year of life was one of weakness and occasional sickness.

The FDA places high importance on manageable side effects of new cancer treatments. Hopefully, more new medications will come that minimize suffering. Researchers have sometimes found substances that get rid of a cancer, only to be derailed by their *toxicity*. I recently visited a Yale patient in her room at Smilow where a new drug in an experimental trial took away her eyesight. Thankfully, it wasn't permanent, but guess what: her cancer went into remission. Potential loss of something so precious as eyesight is enough to permanently kill a promising new treatment, even if it cures the cancer.

I have often wondered: what if a geeky research scientist in his/her secluded lab one day hit upon a substance that would cure all cancer?

The first thing that scientist must do is hire security and a bodyguard. I'm not kidding. Not only would there be a terrific rush of patients, but there could be conglomerates that would stand to lose a ton of money.

Cancer is such a major disease that a whole world of treatment and investment has opened up, unlike that for any other disease in the history of mankind. I think of the "geeky scientist" stumbling on the cure every time I stand on Park Street in New Haven and gawk up high at the new 14-story Smilow Cancer Hospital at Yale. Turn around and across the street there's the Pfizer Clinical Research Unit, showing the close ties between America's medical industrial complex, its pharmaceutical companies, and our hospitals and medical schools.

If science ever found one substance to cure cancer, trillions of dollars of investment in medical infrastructure and human expertise would become irrelevant almost overnight. Yet that is the ultimate treatment goal our society is working towards every day. We all pray it happens.

The good news is we've created the conditions, funding, and training for those thousands of scientists intent on curing cancer. The bad news is cancer treatment remains too high-cost. Two weeks for me as an in-patient at Yale with only an IV-administered treatment (no surgery, no ICU) cost $285,000. My home in Connecticut isn't worth that much. And we're talking *just one* treatment here. I've had five full years of intensive treatment, costing well beyond $1 million. Stories like this are commonplace among all cancer patients. Fortunate for me, my insurance paid what they were supposed to, but my premiums and deductibles now exceed $13,000 annually for me alone, a 57-year-old male. For those 30% of Americans without insurance, the stress of cancer treatment is compounded by their inability of pay for the latest therapies.

～ ～

A most beautiful part of this ugly disease is the team of medical professionals who treat you.

Leah, one of my nurses at NIH in Bethesda, stood at the foot of my bed seeing me curled up in the fetal position. My round-the-clock nausea was unbearable from the chemo NIH was infusing into my body to take down my immune system. Five anti-nausea drugs, wristbands, epidermal patches, and ginger tea—nothing was working. I was suffering. Leah quietly took her hand, reached down, and firmly but gently grasped my leg near the ankle. She held it there for many minutes, silently watching me with genuine compassion. Like magic, the nausea almost disappeared. For the next hour, I felt so much better. A simple nurse's touch eased my pain.

When we cancer patients treasure a particular nurse or doctor, we get anxious when it's their day off and someone else works on us. That's a good measure of their performance.

Today's cancer doctors and nurses put in long hours of training for a disease with such unpredictable outcomes. For doctors, it's about 10-12 years of training and interning. They rack up college tuition bills of over a half million dollars. Today's doctors are at high risk of malpractice lawsuits; one mistake or *perceived* error can sometimes wipe out an entire career. And get this: no longer can they set the prices for their services once they become doctors. Today's doctors are told what they will be paid either by the contract they sign with a hospital, or by an insurance company, or by Medicare/Medicaid.

Understanding all this, I formed a special bond and appreciation with my medical team. They amazed me. Why would *they* choose such a career? Would one of us choose to have humongous student loans for a job where we'd be fighting insurance companies, and our clients could die, and worse they could sue us for the least little thing? You have to be a saint today to want to become a doctor or nurse who treats cancer. You must be gut-driven to help people in their darkest hour.

This system, tortuous as it is, produces the best and the brightest men and women to battle the most feared disease. They have to be outstanding individuals to pass the muster. Every cancer patient should treat them accordingly.

All of a sudden, the thought popped in my mind: call Len. It was a Friday afternoon. He was 100 miles away from me. We were both executive directors of parallel state trade associations, he in Rhode Island, me in Connecticut. He was battling esophageal cancer. I was battling melanoma.

At the precise moment the phone rang in his home, Len was talking about me. His wife laughed when I identified myself. Call it telepathy, or maybe destiny.

Len's voice was labored. "I'm letting go," he told me. My heart sank. "There's nothing more they can do for me. I'm at peace with it. I gave it the good fight. I'm ready to go."

I closed my eyes and swallowed hard with the phone handset tight to my ear. From one cancer patient to another, you would think I had something profound to say, instead I struggled to find the right words.

Len died five days later.

Of all the treatment options afforded cancer patients, the most solemn and peaceful is often the one to stop treatment, or not start it at all.

Many of us have seen it happen to someone we have known. We often don't understand, and it seems to run counter to our human need for self-preservation.

If a patient's prognosis isn't good, he/she may prefer to spend their days doing what they love rather than fighting a battle they think they're unlikely to win.

What is important is that decision be an *informed and educated* decision, I believe. A paramount concern is making the patient's final days as comfortable as possible. The wonderful hospice movement is built around that. The patient needs to know whether a treatment has any chance of remission or prolonging useful life, and what side effects come with it.

Once the cancer patient decides to stop treatment, all around him/her must honor those wishes. It's the one permanent option we all have.

Teams

EVEN BEFORE MY DERMATOLOGIST uttered those first words, "This came back as a malignant melanoma….", teams had already sprung into action on my behalf, unbeknownst to me. I soon realized cancer is a team sport.

My first team was in my dermatologist's office. They rushed that tiny specimen from the top of my scalp to a lab 30 miles away in central Connecticut, where another team of pathology professionals, whom I never met, delved into diagnosing the biopsy.

Receiving the melanoma confirmation from that lab, Dr. Godwin placed his first phone call to Yale surgeon Dr. Ariyan, sowing the seed that branched out like a beautiful plant. In addition to being a dedicated melanoma surgeon, Dr. Ariyan also headed up Yale's melanoma unit, where another team of scientists, researchers, oncologists, and oncology nurses got the notice that a new patient named Bob Heffernan was coming in.

Medical records poured in from my primary care physician and dermatologist. My insurance company got notified and issued clearances. Operating room staff was scheduled. Radiological doctors and staff performed scans. More labs processed blood.

And all of that happened at just the first diagnosis.

With subsequent years of more treatment, many more teams would appear in my future.

Teams that fight cancer are tighter, stronger, and more committed than even the team that wins the Super Bowl. They're on a mission: save this patient's life.

There isn't a wide-angle lens wide enough if I wanted to fit in a single picture my entire cancer team over the past five years. I can easily count over 100 medical professionals who worked for "Team Bob" throughout this period, split evenly between the two primary institutions that treated me: Yale-New Haven and NIH-Bethesda.

My concept of my medical team is far and wide—includes the hospital housekeeping staff, the phlebotomists, the hospital food workers, the administrators, nursing supervisors, medical students, lab techs, dieticians, social workers, and researchers in distant labs analyzing results on my volunteered cancer cells. At least half of them I never met face-to-face, yet they were working to save my life.

"No day is ever routine for *you*," I tell Yale staff when the hospital has me speak to them in orientation and training sessions. "You may think your work is routine, but we as patients see it much differently: we depend so much on *you* to save our lives."

Most health care workers get it, and their lives are truly fulfilled by the sheer goodness of helping patients achieve full health once again. That personal drive leads to wonderful team building

I never missed a chance to praise each and every one of them.

"We'll get the input from the tumor board," my Yale oncologist Dr. Harriet Kluger told me on several occasions.

Every Thursday morning at 7:30am, all Yale-New Haven medical professionals who have anything to do with melanoma gather in a conference room to review all the cases of current patients. There are surgeons, oncologists, nurses, research scientists, pathologists, radiologists, social workers, and their staffs. They pore over labs, scans, surgical results, and swap observations.

The tumor board concept represents the height of team effectiveness. It's used by hospitals across the nation. At Yale, there are tumor boards for lung cancer, another for breast cancer, and so on.

For the patient, it's like getting a team of medical opinion for the price of one. More than once, I would run into another doctor or nurse who already knew my case entirely.

The first time melanoma metastases appeared in my lung, Dr. Kluger felt the right course of action was to surgically remove them. Her intuition was confirmed days later by the opinion of everyone else on the tumor board. My decision to forego some experimental treatment at Yale for the TIL adoptive cell therapy at NIH 300 miles away also got approval by the Yale melanoma tumor board.

For the doctor, the tumor board ratifies or alters a decision through peer review. Sometimes other doctors see a different, more advantageous course to follow. Chances are there would be fewer mistakes and better outcomes for the patient.

Twice a day for the four weeks I was hospitalized in the National Institutes of Health Clinical Center, as many as 20 professionals wearing white lab coats would first stop in the hallway outside the door to my room, then all come in and surround my bed. What a reassuring sight for a stage four cancer patient!

Rounds, the medical establishment calls them. Making the rounds.

But in essence, for cancer patients, they're indispensable to curing or treating the disease. Rounds are essentially team review of the patient's progress.

A lot of listening is the hallmark of rounds. Doctors listen to nurses and medical students, to fellows and interns, to lab techs and to researchers—and vice versa. As the team moves from one patient to another, often trends or patterns emerge that stimulate thinking and problem-solving.

The famous Dr. Steve Rosenberg often stood by my bed during these rounds, indicating their value never diminished for someone so renowned, experienced and wise. Research nurses would take notes. Palliative care therapists would discuss my nausea, and whether those medicines might interfere with the treatment.

Amazingly, they all understand their vital role in the team function.

The path to wellness demands that family members, loved ones, friends, and even fellow patients become essential links in the cancer patient's team.

More hospitals are embracing the practice of *patient and family-centered care*, where the consumers of health care are cherished for their involvement at every level. For instance, when nurses change shifts, the outgoing nurse briefs the incoming nurse on what happened to that patient—but that process is enhanced when it's done at the patient's bedside with his family there to give more information and input. There was a time when doctors' rounds were conducted only outside the patient's room, preventing the patient from hearing what is being said about him or her. Today, more rounds include time for the patient to speak up, or if he/she cannot, his family to speak at the bedside.

There are your medical teams, and your domestic teams. My husband Allen and my Mom, along with the rest of my family formed the nucleus of my domestic team— watching out for my every move, my welfare, my life. My secretary and the leaders of the associations I direct became a team to stand in for me during my absence. Following hospitalization, even the Yale melanoma support group became part of "Team Bob", watching out for me, guiding me, advising me, praying for me.

This part of my cancer team lifted me up spiritually and emotionally.

It all integrates to the benefit of the cancer patient.

So many cancer sufferers sadly choose to go it alone, internalize their struggle, and fail to see the network of beneficence that surrounds them—their team.

When we open our eyes to the extraordinary team that materializes to deal with our cancer, when we appreciate their goodness and selflessness, then can we feel the power to heal and overcome.

Team cancer is always on our side, until they're no longer needed. And until the day when cancer is finally cured, those teams will spring into action over and over again.

Love & Support

INSIDE FABLED STERLING HALL, the focal building of the Yale School of Medicine, along with four other melanoma survivors, we asked for a meeting with key officials of Yale-New Haven Hospital and the medical school about ways to raise the melanoma program to greater prominence.

They turned it into an elegant luncheon. We couldn't help feeling honored. Each of us endured years of treatment. We cared so deeply about the program that was saving our lives, and we knew several ways it could be improved. Yale had an underappreciated jewel in its melanoma program.

We could feel the weight of history as we gazed around the marbled Sterling Hall, a quick walk down Cedar Street from the Hospital. The Yale School of Medicine dates back to 1810, one of the nation's oldest. Students had to be brainy just to qualify for admission. True, this was considered a bastion of "old medicine", but undeniably one of the world's finest training facilities for doctors and research scientists.

On our agenda: grooming an eventual successor melanoma department head to the super-capable Dr. Ariyan, who was past retirement age, retaining key physicians such as my Dr. Kluger, promoting the capabilities of the Yale melanoma program beyond Connecticut's borders, involving patients, and bringing new treatments to Yale such as the TIL Adoptive Cell Therapy at NIH.

That Yale would even listen to us patients signaled how concerned an institution it is. We had the full attention of the CEO and the executive director of Yale's Smilow Cancer Hospital, and the deputy dean of the medical school who also oversaw many of the doctors practicing in the hospital.

But then Mary Russell asked to speak. My beloved fellow melanoma patient, whose TIL treatment experience at NIH put her into full remission and persuaded me to follow, dropped a bombshell.

"You know my husband and I have decided to commit a generous gift to Yale for melanoma research," she said calmly. The total was in the millions of dollars.

Stunned, I almost fell out of my chair. I had no clue she had that kind of wealth to share, despite our three-year friendship as fellow melanoma warriors.

Her fund empowered Yale to focus more on its melanoma research effort, preserving labs, embarking on new projects, and hiring high-powered scientists.

⁂

The love and support for and from cancer patients and their families transcends the normal travails of human life. Cancer inspires us to do things we never, ever thought or dreamed we could do. Cancer magnifies the most lovely human emotions and traits.

Out in the hallway following that meeting, I wrapped my arms around Mary Russell, kissed her and gave her a bear hug. What an exceptional woman! She turned her potentially fatal experience with cancer into a supportive role par none. Humble, warm, understated, she plunged into leading a rich life full of support for others. Her roles include being a clinical psychologist, a professional photographer, cancer patient advocate, and community enrichment.

There are hundreds of thousands of cancer-affected people like Mary Russell in communities across the world who make a difference. You don't have to look far. Down the road from my home is *Ann's Place* in Bethel, Connecticut, where professional staff and clinical volunteers empower cancer survivors to take control of their lives through counseling, education, art therapy, financial assistance, loaning of medical equipment, help with prescriptions, and more. Just over the state line in nearby Purdys, New York, *Friends of Karen* provides emotional, financial and advocacy support to children with life-threatening illness and their families. Would these organizations have risen to this type of support and service had their namesakes not encountered cancer? We'll never know.

Love requires two or more people. Love is the strongest, most unique trait of the human race.

When we get cancer, not only do we receive lots of love, we need it to cope. Cancer brings out the love in all of us.

Cancer is rarely a private disease. Most cancer patients do not have the luxury of suffering their disease in private. Almost always, our family will have to be involved, as will our co-workers, our friends, our community.

From the first diagnosis, I wrestled with how many people to tell and who to tell. Sooner or later, everyone in my life would find out about it. I decided on that 20-minute ride home from the Doctor's first diagnosis not only to reveal it all, but also to open my heart. It was an easy decision, and it was the right decision—because a patient who feels loved can better tackle the tough road ahead, wherever it leads—cure, remission, or end of life.

The love and support a cancer patient gets from friends and family enables strength and courage and comfort. I think back to all those days and nights in the hospital. My Mom and my husband Allen always there, sitting near my bed, touching me, holding me, grasping my hand, kissing me, loving me. Their love and support propped me up like the two-foot thick stone foundation at my home in Connecticut. They provided the psychological crutch that held fear in check, that made life worth living, and that pushed me to seek daring, difficult treatments.

Thanks to the family and medical leave law, Allen could be with me for the entire four weeks I was hospitalized at NIH without losing his job. The three associations that I'm executive director of allowed me to take off a combined total of several months over five years for treatment, an extremely supportive act of care and concern.

Love for me poured into me in so many ways. Aunt Annie demanded to drive me to and from infusion treatments. I discovered that people around me are honored to help me. They want to be there for me. There was a steady stream of love in the form of cards, letters, flowers, plants, fruit baskets, phone calls, e-mails, prepared meals, and visitors.

Steve Jones's face showed anxiety. It was his first visit to the Yale melanoma support group. Amazing to me that despite never having seen this man, I could read into his body language the strain he was under.

Young (early 40s) and handsome with two young boys and a beautiful wife, he was in the fight of his life with melanoma tumors in his lungs and liver. Yale had thrown several treatments at him, but his tumors kept growing. Yale's Dr. Ariyan had done an admirable job removing a portion of Steve's left facial jaw area where the cancer first appeared, and rebuilt it so you could hardly tell.

Cancer patients never know what to expect from a support group. Some avoid them fearing the troubles of other sufferers will only depress them further. Some are afraid of opening up and exposing themselves to strangers.

But many patients flourish in the support group setting. Steve's one visit that night to our group probably saved his life. He came into the room wondering if he was going to die. He left full of hope and new knowledge, with the loving encouragement of fellow patients.

As we probed him for past therapies and current cancer staging, I started thinking Steve was a perfect candidate for the TIL procedure at NIH. He was in excellent health, he had tumors of a large enough size, and previous treatments had failed.

"Bob, tell him about TIL," gestured our melanoma buddy Mark Driggs. "TIL cleared the cancer for both Bob and Mary Russell. Maybe it would work for you," he told Steve.

Steve listened intently. He left that night with a smile.

Maybe there was another option for him. We shared the same Yale oncologist—Harriet Kluger—who wanted to try one last trial drug on him. Several months later when it too failed, Dr. Kluger asked if I could say a few words in support of Steve's referral to NIH with the doctors there. They immediately admitted Steve to the TIL trial and found his TIL cells were so vigorous they grew twice as many in the NIH lab as were grown for me. He easily aced the four-week TIL procedure, and it began to work. All of his tumors disappeared within two months, except for one, and that too shrunk more with every check-up.

At support group meetings, we patients can get down dirty and honest. We can say things patients never will hear from physicians, but still need to be told. We make connections and friendships lasting beyond the monthly group meetings.

I'm fond of claiming 50% of all I know about my cancer was gleaned from fellow patients. It's true. There's nothing more authentic than the experience of a fellow patient. Their experiences become empowering for other patients. We can point out hopeful avenues, or we can frankly warn against doing something futile.

Lee Banks, an athletic, devoted soccer player in his early 50s, came confidently to one of our support group meetings. "They found a few mets in the brain, they'll nuke 'em with the gamma knife, and I should be set to go," he told the rest of us.

I swallowed hard and kept uncharacteristically close-mouthed on hearing Lee's overconfidence. I knew something

Lee obviously didn't: he might not have long to live. That was so devastating I couldn't bring myself to say it to him in front of the other patients. We had lost four other melanoma patients in our two-year-old support group to brain mets.

During the 75-minute drive home from New Haven to New Milford, Allen and I debated the entire ride how to handle the Lee Banks situation. While the gamma knife might indeed clear the cancer, the fact was his chances were extraordinarily slim.

"I don't want to come out and say, 'Lee, you're gonna die'," I argued with Allen. "But someone's got to tell him he might not have much time." It was a classic case where a patient could come say something the doctor probably wouldn't.

The next morning I composed a gingerly worded e-mail to Lee. "Have you asked your Doctor exactly how successful the gamma knife is on brain mets?," I said to him.

He replied promptly, "Maybe you know something I don't?" Lee asked to meet with me one-on-one, where I urged him to live like every day was his last.

Lee Banks died less than a year later. At his funeral, I promised his wife Ruth I would advocate for melanoma brain met patients whenever I could, and proceeded to do just that at subsequent research conferences.

Angels

My Grammie watches over me.

At least one Angel watches over all cancer patients. Whether or not you believe in forces beyond our daily human existence, it's harmless and actually beneficial to believe in Angels. That power and love of someone you held close in your heart who has passed on can transcend the dimensions to care for you the rest of your life.

To this day, I can still feel her tears running down my cheek. Gram stood in the breezeway of her Bristol, Vermont home that cool Monday morning in July, waiting to give me one last hug and kiss before I went out the door for the 230-mile drive back to Connecticut. My 94-year-old Grandmother often had watery eyes every time she said good-bye to me in her long life, but this morning her tears gushed out onto my face as I hugged her frail little body.

"Love you, my Grammie," I said as we rocked in a tight embrace. "Love you, too," she sobbed, as if she knew it was our last living moment together. I hated living so far away from her.

Five-and-a-half hours later, just as I arrived in the parking lot of my Connecticut office, the call came over the cell phone: she had been rushed to the hospital with a stroke. Immediately, I turned around the car for an emergency trip straight back to Vermont. She died later that afternoon before I could get to her bedside.

Something told me to go to Vermont that third weekend of July 2007. I don't know what it was. I had so much work to catch up on. But cancer had given me the power to say, "Screw the work and enjoy life."

So, I packed my bags and traveled to what would become one of the most memorable weekends of my life. I made breakfast for Gram, Mom and Aunt Annie. We went out to lunch. As we did so often, Gram and I sat on a couch holding hands and talked and talked.

We went to Shelburne Museum that Sunday, wheeling Gram in and out of 30 exhibition buildings where she told tour guides more about living in historic Vermont than they knew.

Gram loved to ride around her beloved native state. On the way back from Shelburne, she had me turn on some country road that took us home a way I'd never been, past Monkton Pond. All the while, she was telling stories about what happened here and there, and stories of who lived in this house and that one. I so regret not recording all her precious recollections, told from a crystal-clear memory.

She knew I had cancer, and visited me in Yale after one of my surgeries and several doctor appointments. The dedication of a grandmother prompted this 90-plus-year-old to make the long trip. Strangely, she didn't appear as fearful and emotional about my disease as I expected she would be. Looking back, I now wonder if she knew something I didn't.

Some higher power, some keen intuition guided me to enjoy one final weekend with my Grammie. As we said our final good-byes that Monday morning, little did I know that she was blessing me with her beautiful Angel tears.

In her life and beyond, she would be by my side throughout my cancer-fighting years.

No grandson and grandmother ever had a tighter bond than ours. She was set up to be my Angel from the start.

Days after I was born in December 1955, my Mom brought her first child home to live in Gram's house in New Haven Mills, Vermont. At the time, my Dad was a military serviceman in the U.S. Air Force, stationed overseas in Europe. Not having a real income, Mom had no choice but to start raising me in my grandparent's home.

I was also the *first* grandchild. Hey, what kid wouldn't relish a monopoly on the love and attention of his Mom, Gram, Gramp, and three uncles for the first year of his life? OK, you could say I was spoiled, but I did return all that love back in spades. More than anything else, that first year of my life glued my Grammie and I together. It was a natural and deep love—so much so that when I converse with other people, I say that one of life's greatest gifts are your grandparents. Throughout my childhood years, I would cry every time we drove away from Gram's house, looking out the rear view window of the car at her and Gramp waving goodbye. Seemed like we were together every other weekend, no matter the long distance that separated us nor the years that aged us.

～

Luella B. Cooke Masse Sumner Washburn could have taught many cancer patients about strength and survivorship.

Gram's life was hard in the mountains of central Vermont, growing up on subsistence farms in the 1920s and 1930s. If you didn't grow it, raise it, or preserve it, you didn't eat. Jobs were tough to find. The winters were brutally cold and snowy, offset only by wood heat. She had to ride her horse, Dolly, down Bristol Notch and up the valley to attend school.

Gram's first husband abandoned her and their three young children. She worked 40 years in a garment factory, never earning more than $46 a week. Her second husband, with whom she bore her fourth child, worked hard to raise the whole family, but would become an alcoholic in later years, dragging Gram back into poverty during retirement. Often, I would send her checks to help out. Through it all, Gram never lost her dignity. She somehow maintained a home and dressed like she was worth millions. She outlived a third husband who died of cancer, with whom she enjoyed several nice years.

And then, at age 89, a coronary bypass surgery nearly killed her, but she persevered and left the hospital four months later, living another five good years before our fateful departure that July morning.

I feel Gram's guiding presence every time I endure a cancer treatment or get test results. She's there. I can almost smell her fragrant perfume. I can feel her bony arthritic fingers on my shoulder. She's shaking her head affirmatively and smiling: *everything will be all right.*

If she suddenly appeared in a white gown with wings, I swear to you I would not be surprised. Honestly. But my Grammie's style wouldn't have her wearing all white.

Angels don't fit a mold. They emanate from loved ones who may not have been entirely perfect on this earth. But cancer survivors can feel their beneficence and potency.

In my two major cancer surgeries following her death, I could just close my eyes and envision Grammie inside the operating room. The comfort I feel is overwhelming and powerful. She's there with many other loved ones who have passed away—my Aunt Charlotte whose liver cancer took her in 1980, my friend Karen who succumbed to brain cancer, my Uncle Bob who didn't survive throat cancer, my Dad who died of a heart attack at a young age in 1982, and on and on. Yes, sometimes Angels work in teams.

"Be with me, Gram," I often tell myself as I go into the CT scanner. "Be with me," murmured again as I go into the MRI tube. "Be with me, Gram," as I wait full of anxiety in the doctor's exam room for the test results.

Now, mind you, you're hearing this from a man who's never been very religious. I've never believed in the supernatural. Before suffering cancer, if someone told me they believed in angels, I would have politely smiled and said, "Whatever comforts you, good for you."

Angels are your very own personal force who can

miraculously put you on a path to wellness or peace. What have you got to lose? Believe in the Angels that watch over you. We all have them. They're there. It took cancer to make me see this.

My Grammie watches over me. Her unending love and devotion sustain me. So far, she's working wonders for me. She is my Angel.

Dreams

MOST DREAMS ARE FORGOTTEN over time. This one was too powerful for a cancer patient to forget.

In the NIH intensive care unit, I was returning to consciousness from anesthesia following major surgery—my fourth cancer operation. Thoracic surgeons had cut an 18-inch incision in my back to retrieve a tumor lodged between my right lung and the esophagus.

In those groggy moments as I looked around my ICU suite and tried to get my bearings, I suddenly remembered this dream I had somewhere in the surgical process. My eyes watered up and a big smile came across my face.

The dream placed me in an audience. I could see many people sitting around me. There were rows of people all chatting merrily. Looking around this mythical setting, I could see flowers arranged seemingly everywhere. For a moment I wondered if this was a funeral, but then I looked again at the audience. Some of the women wore pretty hats and corsages. At the front of this room, there were gorgeous, large standing floral displays. From my 19 years running a flower shop, I knew these were flowers of a celebration.

Relieved, I assured myself this was no funeral.

In the dream I turned my head to the left. There was an aisle running up the middle, decorated with more flowers, and tulle, and big fluffy bows. It was so beautiful and peaceful.

Suddenly, this bride in a flowing white gown and veil floated by down the aisle. Her pure blond hair softly blew in the air as she went by. She was holding colorful flowers for a bouquet. As I looked into her face, it was my niece, Jolee.

"Phew! Wow," I muttered to myself back in the ICU, recalling with utter joy this wonderful gift of a dream at such a tough moment in my battle with cancer. I had to lift my arm, heavy with IVs, to my face and wipe a tear off my cheek.

What made this dream so incredibly powerful, is that my adorable niece Jolee Heffernan was just four years old that day enjoying a kid's life at her home in Middlebury, Vermont.

The subconscious mind, from which most dreams emanate, had reassured her Uncle Bob that he might triumph over cancer in this battle of his life to witness Miss Jolee's wedding 20+ years into the future.

Five months later, I recounted the dream to a roomful of melanoma research scientists and medical doctors at Yale-New Haven Hospital and the Yale Medical School. They were there to share and review each other's highly technical cancer research projects. Most of their science was way above my laymen's brain, focused on genetic and immunological approaches to defeating cancer. I was there as a patient advocate, to bring that unique perspective only a cancer survivor could communicate.

As I told my Jolee dream to these brainy PhDs and MDs, the room fell silent. It was a moment of human emotion that these men and women of science rarely encountered in their labs and technical experiments. I could see several of them swallow the hard lumps in their throats.

"Well, I guess this means you're going to beat the cancer," suggested Yale's Dr. Mario Sznol, breaking the awkward silence.

I patted him on the shoulder with a big smile. "Wouldn't that be great?"

"All of you in this room made that dream possible," I told these eminent researchers, trying to look each one of them in the face. "Certainly, the NIH researchers made it possible. There I was, in the world's largest medical research hospital, undergoing a wild new cancer therapy. The entire experience was made possible by people like you."

"All of you dream about finding cures for cancer. We patients dream about getting cures and returning to a normal life," I said.

Some practitioners of integrative medicine use dreams of cancer patients to integrate healing imagery with other forms of treatment. History tells us that Hippocrates, the Father of Modern Medicine, used dream therapy and encouraged patients to harness healing dreams. They not only can predict the course of an illness, they can also give us the power to change the course of our disease. And of course, dreams often reveal a truth we are otherwise unable to accept or admit or see.

To all cancer patients, here's my advice: harness the power of your dreams.

Tears

OFF FLEW MY PATIENT scrubs when the NIH doctor told me that Sunday afternoon my white cell count was high enough they could let me outside the NIH hospital in Bethesda on a temporary pass. Three weeks cooped up inside a hospital with little immunity is enough to give anyone the worst cabin fever.

Excited but weak, I threw on a sweat suit and sneaks. The nurses smiled and waved me off with a friendly warning, "Be careful and take it easy." They knew I wasn't physically able to go very far and would return the next morning.

Downstairs, the cavernous NIH Hatfield Clinical Center lobby was nearly empty as daytime turned into evening.

"I think I better take the shuttle," I said to Allen & Mom. Looking to left outside the lobby entrance, the Safra Lodge stood a short walk away. I knew I couldn't make it, or at least I ought not to try.

A blast of cool March air hit me as Allen opened the door.

"No, wait," I ordered Allen & Mom to stop. My lungs sucked in huge gasps of the fresh outdoor air. It was beautifully dense, cold, and rich in fresh oxygen. A light mist fell outside. I didn't want to move, taking in one deep breath after another with long, wonderful exhales. Three weeks of inpatient care left me with a renewed appreciation for the beauty of fresh air.

"It feels so good!" I exclaimed to Allen as he rolled his eyes upward. "We take this SO for granted." My partner cared more about me catching a cold with a severely weakened immune system than my newfound love for fresh air. "Let's go," Allen ordered me.

A mom and dad with their young 10-year-old son, bald from a cancer treatment, hopped aboard the shuttle bus along with us. We smiled at each other in the brotherhood of knowing what each other was going through. I flashed thumbs up, which he heartily returned. Across the driveway stood another outstanding free hotel for NIH patients and families, the Children's Lodge.

Inside the Safra Lodge moments later, I felt elated entering something that felt close to the home environment. Built with private monies only five years earlier, Safra had 37 sleeping rooms like the nicest hotels. The main floor housed elegant wood-paneled rooms and furniture, a library, living room with fireplace, and huge state-of-the art kitchen for guests to cook as if they were home.

"I can do the stairs," I assured Mom as Allen raced ahead of us to open the sleeping room. Out of breath at the top of two flights, I plunked in a group of sofas that created another lounge area on the second floor.

Without warning, my eyes watered up. Light became wavy as I looked around. Then tears gushed down my cheeks. I started to sob and couldn't control it. It just went on and on. Mom wrapped her arms around me and hugged me tightly.

This was my breakdown and I deserved every minute

of it. A long four years of potential mortality and battle extraordinaire culminated in this moment: four major surgeries, one year of Interferon, eight weeks of hospital treatment, two weeks of IL-2, over 25 CT scans and brain MRIs, countless blood tests and IV infusions. Four years plus of simply not knowing where it would all lead, of worry, pain, and intermittent nausea.

"I need a good cry, Mom. I'm sorry." It had also been four years of trying to be strong for my mother. No parent should ever have to see their child endure cancer, whatever their age.

"You've been through so much," she tried to console me.

An hour later after composing myself, I had the harebrained idea to start calling friends and family from Allen & Mom's room inside the Safra Lodge.

A call to my cousin Dee and Carol to tell them I would probably attend their wedding the following Saturday in Connecticut turned into another tearful mush.

A call to my Godmother in Vermont unleashed more tears.

More calls, more attempts to talk came in a broken voice. Ever tried to stifle tears in a phone call? It doesn't work.

Plain and simple, my heart was overjoyed at making it all the way through the TIL treatment—against all the odds and risks. There still was no guarantee my new cells would get rid of the cancer. The months and years ahead would slowly reveal that.

Never deprive a cancer patient of his or her tears.

Hard to explain, but in all my years of battling cancer, I've shed only *tears of joy*. I never once cried when I got bad news or when scared.

Crying can catch even the most stoic person off guard. Experts see crying as an emotional response to certain feelings, usually sadness and hurt. But more important, crying serves the psychological purpose of releasing built-up feelings. There's a body of science that believes crying may have a biochemical purpose to release stress hormones or toxins from the body.

Many months after my TIL treatment, I got up the nerve to announce my progress against cancer in church during the *Joys & Sorrows* portion of the service. In the car on the way, I had it all rehearsed calmly and logically. The moment I stood up and started talking, my voice broke: "I'm thankful to the people of America for funding groundbreaking medical research that might have saved my life…..". I barely made it through the talk.

Cancer so beautifully enables patients and their families to cry and express a host of emotions where normally they operate socially as unemotional stalwarts.

And for the record, we male cancer patients cry just as much as the women.

Victories

MOST OF US HATE war and would rather have peace. But we're all enlisted in the battle against cancer. That's one war everybody can agree must be waged. It's also one we don't want to lose.

Almost everyday, we need victories in our lives. That feeling of winning and the high that goes with is often associated with sports, or with winning an election, or a successful business venture. The victory mentality empowers us to move forward, reach higher, and try things we otherwise might avoid.

After that moment when a doctor pronounces, "You have cancer", the road becomes bumpy, curvy, and hilly. Along the way, there will almost certainly be victories of all sizes, some huge, some tiny. Considering the stress a cancer warrior undergoes, each win, no matter how small, can be a big emotional lift up. Even the little wins can help us get through the "down" days when we feel yucky, or get dreaded bad news.

I am a cancer survivor, and I choose to focus on and appreciate any and all victories that come my way, no matter how small:

- a "good" blood test

- a day without diarrhea
- breathing well after lung surgery in recovery
- a CT scan that's good (I like to hear the word "clear")
- "NED" (no evidence of disease)
- getting your energy back
- a CT scan where tumors are "rock solid stable"
- hungry, feel like eating
- simply a day of feeling like yourself, close to normal, of feeling good
- no pain
- an MRI of the brain showing no metastases
- discharged from the hospital (there's no place like home)
- insurance agreeing to cover your medical treatments
- a comfortable IV needle stick and placement
- no nausea
- delicious hospital food
- regaining your sense of taste (Coca-Cola tastes like Coke again)
- the tumor grew "just a little"
- your favorite nurse on duty
- mild side effects
- no side effects
- a comfortable hospital bed
- being able to take a nice warm shower during treatment
- your port or catheter coming out

- longer periods between scans & doctor appointments
- feeling good enough to have visitors
- a treatment ending early
- finishing a treatment
- no complications or infections
- sleeping soundly
- a private hospital room
- more days without anxiety
- incisions healing well
- drains coming out
- going to the bathroom on your own
- coming out of ICU
- coming out of isolation
- taking a long walk (with or without your IV pole)
- all the organs working normally, together
- your hair growing back, in all the right places
- a good, well-deserved cry
- able to drive your car again
- looking in the mirror and smiling
- gaining your weight back
- smiling & joking again
- able to have sex again

Victories for this cancer patient can come in many shapes and sizes. Each one is precious in its own way.

Some victories are more momentous.

Keeping the cancer patient comfortable in his/her

waning days is a major victory in itself. Nobody wins when there is suffering.

End of life, on the patient's own terms, surrounded by family and loved ones, is the height of compassionate care and personal dignity.

The greatest victory of all: passing time without a recurrence of cancer. As I write this, I am three years out from the TIL treatment at NIH. There are no new tumors. Doesn't matter whether it's six months, one year, two years, or seven years. We cancer patients keep track of milestones. We earned those victories, and they're all ours.

Camaraderie

THERE'S A SPECIAL, BEAUTIFUL bond between cancer patients, survivors, and their families. Perhaps it derives out of our shared experiences. Cancer creates a special compassion that crosses all human boundaries.

I felt it that first Monday in June 2007 when I walked into the Yale infusion center to start a year's treatment with Interferon. Looking around the complex, I saw at least 30 patients in cancer's obvious grasp: hairless men and women, some of them children, ashen skin color, and bodies that had lost too much weight. Their IV poles stood proudly next to them, dripping liquid hope into their veins. Nurses and doctors kept monitoring them, changing the tubes and plumbing that goes with chemotherapy infusion. Each chair reclined with a personal TV screen attached to a long, moveable suspension arm.

But almost every patient—no matter how sick—flashed me a smile or a nod.

"This chair's empty, go ahead and sit here," I remember one man trying to welcome me as if it was his living room. Indeed, it really was his *living* room. The infusion center was full of life and hope.

I swallowed a hard lump seeing all the families and loved ones sitting stoically next to each patient. They tended to needs, such as a warming blanket for the ever-cold cancer patient, or finding something appetizing for them in the infusion center's refrigerator like yogurt or jello. I could see their love and determination to stand by or sit by with firm support.

Stories were flying back and forth across the infusion ward. "Now, what's your cancer?" "When were you first diagnosed?" "What chemo do they have you on?" As the patient in the reclining chair would doze off, the families would keep the conversation going in whispers. "He's gone through hell, but we think he's going to make it." "How do you get them to eat more?" "How's he managing the side effects?"

As days wore on that first month, I recognized more "buddies", friends we made sitting together the usual three or four hours it took for the course of treatment.

One day, I began to lose my sense of taste from the treatment. Coca-cola tasted like water to me. "Switch to root beer or Dr. Pepper," another patient suggested. Great advice! We patients were looking out for each other.

A young woman in her late 20s frequented the infusion chairs, her body wasted away from advanced ovarian cancer that had spread. I felt so much concern for her, wondering if she would survive. One day when she wasn't there, her regular nurse took a phone call steps away from my chair, which I couldn't avoid overhearing. From the conversation, I easily deduced the young woman was at the other end of the call. "No, please don't worry about the sugar content in the ice cream," the nurse said into the phone. "You just need to get as much food into you as you can." In one of the most human moments I've ever witnessed, the nurse ended the call by standing with her back to us patients for several minutes more staring out the window overlooking Long Island Sound, wiping tears from her eyes, and composing herself before turning to face her next patient.

Interestingly, when Yale built the new Smilow Cancer Hospital, the new infusion chairs were designed for more privacy. But many if not most of us patients fondly remember the sharing and camaraderie of the infusion ward set-up. The older infusion center I started treatment in had private rooms for those who wanted them, but I noticed they were usually empty. Instinctively, all of us wanted to be together.

For the next three years, during my monthly clinic visits to that top floor of the former Yale Cancer Center complex at Long Wharf in New Haven, I always wandered back into the infusion center, smiling in solidarity at new patients in the chairs. We were all in the fight against cancer *together*—a bond that no one could put asunder.

Screw HIPPA, I decided early on. I didn't care one hoot who knew about my disease. By sharing, I could help other patients and their experience could help me. That was my choice and I have been so much the better for it.

The *Health Insurance Portability and Accountability Act* passed into law in 1996 to protect, in part, patient privacy. It's been a good law, by and large, but sometimes it works against building relationships among cancer patients, which can be so valuable to wellness and healing. Some doctors and hospitals have gone overboard in erecting barriers to sharing because of HIPPA, fearing liability. The law has succeeded in creating a culture of secrecy among health care professionals and institutions. For example, I was forever proud to see "YUHEF" in scientific presentations of melanoma researchers. It stood for my cell line: "YU" meaning Yale University, and "HEF" being the first three letters of my last name. Then, one day, a Yale legal official told me "YUHEF" was a too-descriptive identifier that had to be changed to something less decipherable. Give me a break.

I'll always regret how I fell victim to the HIPPA mentality in one case. Walking into the infusion center one day, the sight of Norman Wellings in a chair surprised me. For a very awkward three hours, we didn't talk to each other save for the cordial "hello" and "take care." Norm was a prominent member of one of my trade associations that I managed whom I deeply respected, and who was always praising my work for his industry. He obviously didn't know if he should say something, given my notoriety as head of a major industry in the state of Connecticut. Conversely, our business relationship bolted my tongue—highly unusual and out of character for me. He died almost one year later of pancreatic cancer. I'm left feeling remorseful about not reaching out to him. It has spurred me to connect with more cancer colleagues for the good of us all.

Memo to all current and future cancer warriors: HIPPA is there to protect us. But we can elect to tear down the wall and open ourselves to the beauty and benefit of sharing. We cannot have compassion for someone if we don't know how they're suffering.

At one time in my younger life, I'm not proud to admit, I would see a cancer patient out in public with the bald head-sickly-look and think, "shouldn't they stay at home?" Well, where you stand is where you sit. Having cancer or loving someone who has it changes your whole perspective. Today, I might walk up to that same person, softly pat him or her on the back, and introduce myself: "stage four melanoma, and a *survivor!*"

Cancer patients have the tightest fraternity. My "second Mom" Phyllis finally caved in to my constant prodding and joined a breast cancer support group in Burlington, Vermont the last year of her life. Living home alone, she needed the input of other women who knew exactly what she was going through.

Cancer is an equal-opportunity disease. I'm a gay guy, and I got melanoma. I have helped several conservative, evangelical melanoma patients who oppose the very same sex marriage that united my husband Allen and I. Cancer doesn't discriminate against gay or straight, black or white, woman or man, child or adult, rich or poor, Catholic or Unitarian. It becomes a unifying force that cuts across all of humanity. Cancer helps build bridges for common ground between people who otherwise would never think of cooperating intimately.

I began developing close relationships by freely communicating with fellow cancer warriors around the nation and the world, without regard to their place in the world. The great contribution of the Internet is drawing closer people of the planet with similar struggles in life. Imagine this: just 25 years ago when the World Wide Web was in its infancy, patients of like disease could connect only through local networks hosted mainly by their treatment centers, based on a paper notice or a nurse's recommendation. Today, I can carry on a conversation about melanoma with other patients anywhere in the world. My only limitation is understanding their language, and there are web translators for that too.

I posted my story touting the TIL adoptive cell treatment in several places: Australia's melanoma.au web site, the Melanoma Research Alliance, the Melanoma Research Foundation, Aim at Melanoma on Facebook, American Academy of Dermatology, and the Melanoma Foundation of New England. It's not unusual that I receive as many as five or six contacts each week about people entering stage three or four melanoma. It's so fulfilling to help each of them.

I gave two young Australian melanoma activists—Jay Allen and Clint Heal—a personal tour of Yale's treatment and research facilities. Sergo from Prague in the Czech Republic appealed for help with his stage four lung metastases. Mike from Nova Scotia found new direction for his melanoma after getting in touch with me, and then I provided key information for his doctors on the island, which were not in the loop for latest treatments. I helped Brad, a young carpenter from South Carolina, get into the TIL program at NIH in Bethesda after listening to his status and convincing the NIH team he was a good candidate. John, a fireman from Utah, benefitted from the tip sheet I wrote about the challenges he would face undergoing the same treatment. For Stephanie in Dallas, I sadly confirmed what she didn't want to hear: her mother's brain mets were so serious she probably could not enter the TIL treatment.

We assume it's important to get second opinions about our cancer from two or more doctors. Consider this: opinions from fellow patients who've been there might be more authentic and equally consequential.

All I did was open my heart and my mind to share what I knew with total strangers enduring my disease. That wonderful sense of camaraderie has empowered my own personal sense of wellbeing and healing. It's exhilarating to help another human being find a path to longer, more enjoyable healthy life.

Positive

NOT LONG AFTER YALE started treating me, the doctors and social workers were asking *me* if I wouldn't mind talking to other melanoma patients.

"Joe is in room 6 and is very anxious," Dr Kluger told me during one monthly visit to the medical oncology clinic. "Would you talk to him?"

"Of course," I smiled.

I found Joe to be around my age, mid-50s, sitting there with his wife. He had lost an eye to ocular melanoma, and Dr. Kluger had just given him the dreaded diagnosis that there were now melanoma tumors in his lung. He certainly had enough to be down about.

Simply listening, patient-to-patient, is so therapeutic. I let Joe tell me his story of where the disease had taken him. And now *this*, lung mets, he said dejectedly. His wife stiffened her back, clenched her jaw, trying to be strong in a tough moment.

"Well, let me tell you, last July I had lung surgery to remove my mets," I told Joe. "I worried it would be hard on me, but it turned out to be the easiest of my three cancer surgeries. I woke up in recovery breathing beautifully on my own. Expected to be hooked up to a respirator. That never happened. Can you believe, they sent me home the next day!"

"And best of all, that surgery has given me three clear CT scans—almost a full year!"

"And you still will have so many options after your lung surgery," I urged. "They've got these cool immunology drugs that are close to approval. There's the TIL procedure at NIH. Who knows, Joe, you might have a less aggressive form of the cancer. There are patients here who've had lung mets removed and they never had another recurrence."

"AND, you landed in one of the world's best places to be treated for melanoma—Yale. You may not be in as much trouble as you think," I counseled him.

Joe and his wife needed that positive lift. They each forced a smile and thanked me.

With the high-powered life I had endured, I was always an "up" person. It became a self-imposed psychological tool.

At age 17, I was positive that leaving Connecticut to study journalism in Washington D.C. at an expensive private university for a blue-collar student with no major scholarships was the right path. That risky decision led to a seven-year career on the United States Senate staff, where my can-do spirit and timing of luck led to a key role in putting the Secretary of Education in the President's Cabinet. I just knew I could tackle the immense job of writing a book about that historical endeavor. When tragedy hit my family, I was sure my mother and I could rebuild by running a small business for 19 years. We did, successfully. For many of those years, I also served as executive director of three state nonprofit associations—simultaneously with the business.

And when cancer struck, every positive cell in my body would be enlisted in the fight.

I remember the very first visit with my Yale oncologist, Dr. Kluger. "Stay positive," she warned. "We've done studies on that here at Yale. It helps keep your immune system up. We're going to need that." That turned out to be prophetic advice.

$\sim$

My good doctor didn't have to tell me to "stay positive". Mentally, I was already there.

A cancer patient hears "be positive" so much it becomes a mantra. We hear it from our friends, from our families, from the news media, from a slew of self-help books. But doctors, scientists, and patients are becoming increasingly aware of the connection between mind and body. The mind of an upbeat cancer patient can be powerful tool in the battle against cancer.

The science of the positive mind so intrigued one former NIH researcher, Candace Pert, that she is widely credited with discovering the opiate receptor, the cellular binding site for endorphins in the brain. Her work in the 1980s revealed the unique biochemical communication network between the body and the mind. Author of the book *Molecules of Emotion*, Dr. Pert has also written over 250 scientific articles on peptides and their receptors and the role of these neuropeptides in the immune system. Neuropeptides are molecular messengers that connect *all* systems of the body—including the immune system.

Our emotions are direct-wired to the rest of the body. If we've got cancer and we're convinced we're going to die, we probably will. In this sad state, our mind signals to the body "the end is near." We get depressed, we feel lousy and defeated.

Think of the times in our life when something trying or traumatic happened, and soon after we came down with a bad cold or other illness.

A melanoma patient in our support group at Yale told us her amazing story of how she dealt with stage three melanoma as a young adult woman just prior to her marriage and raising a family. Twenty-four years later, following the tragic, emotional loss of her mother, the melanoma returned in the exact same spot on her body. It's a good bet her immune system held the cancer in check until a mental strain weakened it.

Among the research performed in the past 40 years, being positive has been shown to help the average patient in several ways:

- Enhance the neutrophils, those white cells often called the first line of defense in the immune system,
- Improve the functioning of chemotherapy. Sometimes chemo weakens a cancer enough that the immune system can better respond.
- Reduce the stresses of cancer surgery and speed healing after surgery.
- Augment the numbers of white cells and hormones that assist the immune system.

I took on cancer with the gusto of conquering an exciting challenge, not the fear of a forbidding threat. I decided that I had to set the tone of how my whole attitude towards the disease will rule my every day.

That first day of diagnosis, after composing myself from the initial shock, I actually looked forward to the treatment regimen. Sort of like, let's get this ball rolling!

During that full year of Interferon infusions and injections, I practiced constant imagery. I would close my eyes and envision the drug stimulating my immune system to chase after the cancer cells, one-by-one, then attacking them. It was much like a video game, except the screen was my imagination.

When CT scans showed—twice—the cancer had reached my lung, I *empowered* my surgeons to do what they had to do.

I boosted my positive energy repeatedly by staying in close contact with my medical team, reading up on latest medical developments, and helping other melanoma patients. I've empowered myself by being of service to others. I relished the role of being a patient advocate.

One patient I knew avoided the TIL treatment at NIH, even though she was a perfect candidate, because she worried it was "too toxic." Her outlook and decision probably prevented her from receiving the one and only therapy that could have cured her.

At NIH, my 67 billion new TIL cells flowed into a warm and welcoming body, with me cheering them on during the 30 minutes it took to infuse into them my catheter. To this day, I can see they are still working like little beavers: there are white spots on my skin where they have attacked the melanin in my skin, because it has the biological marker of melanoma.

Once we, the cancer patient, make the decision to pursue a course of treatment—and it is 100% *our decision*—we should embrace it with every ounce of strength and hope. We must be convinced it will work. We must believe in it.

It is possible one day this cancer may still take my life, but certainly not without a valiant fight mobilized by the power of positive thinking and action.

It's just as important to be positive for those around me, I believe.

Much is demanded of cancer patients in summoning herculean strength to maintain their own confidence when cancer saps their own personal stamina. How can we expect them to boost the spirits of our families and friends too?

My Mom and husband Allen worried intensely about me. We can read each other's faces and body language. Hard to hide the anxiety and fear.

Some people want us, the cancer patient, to "be positive" because it makes *their lives* easier. My good friend Dave, an auto mechanic, avoided me and was visibly uncomfortable when I talked about my treatment. Some insulate themselves psychologically from the pain of watching *us* suffer. Everybody responds differently, and that's just the way it is. People don't take coping courses for friends and families dealing with cancer of loved ones.

"You're so positive," people have told me time and again. "You have such a good attitude." At first, I thought there were being courteous. But as I encountered more cancer patients, I could see how many patients could help themselves by adopting a more buoyant approach to their disease. Admittedly, it's not easy. We enable those around us to remain involved in our life when we're positive. They are more energetic players in our support team. We feel better, they feel better, and the whole thing fuels wellness.

As a cancer patient, I felt I had a duty to be positive for my medical team, above all else.

Doctors, nurses, technicians, support crews….they're human beings with feelings. Too often, we expect them to be consistently "up" and bubbly for us, as if we're the only case in their practice. They've chosen a career to help people where outcomes lead to death more than many other diseases. They could have opted for dentistry or optometry where no one ever dies. Yet they chose oncology with all the stressors and emotional encumbrances that go with it.

On a typical day, an oncologist might see 24 patients or more.

Stand in their shoes. In one exam room, a patient is emotionally distraught, depressed, and convinced he won't survive. In the next exam room, the patient is upbeat, enthusiastic for the next treatment, cheering on the doctor and nurse.

Who would you rather work with?

It's elemental human nature that all of us want to be on the winning team. We would rather work with the winners than the losers. I think the positive cancer patient will get better care from their medical team. Sure, the Hippocratic oath requires Doctors to treat all patients equally. But so long as doctors and nurses are human beings and not robots, they will inevitably go the extra mile for the cancer patient who wants to live, and who espouses that positive, strong hope that together they will prevail.

There's one caveat: I've told many doctors it's impossible for a cancer patient to have hope when he or she is suffering. We simply cannot be positive when we are in constant pain and suffering. Since we all know positivity promotes healing, the strategy has to get patients to a level of comfort for that hope and confidence to reign supreme.

I'm positive that's the right approach!

Perspective

ON THE WAY TO my first appointment with melanoma surgeon Dr. Ariyan, I stopped to do a live radio show related to my work. As executive director of three state associations, I often do three or four news media interviews in a typical week.

Not a good idea, this particular day. Probably should have canceled the appearance. On sitting in the studio with headphones, my mind went blank as the host opened her show. I couldn't remember the topic of the show. Of course, it didn't help that the hour-long ride to the studio consumed my mind with cancer. *Would it hurt? Would I survive? Would I be out of work for long?* My thoughts just raced on and on.

20 minutes later I sat in Dr. Ariyan's office. He coolly described how much skin and scalp tissue would be excised from my head, and how the surgery might be expanded to take lymph nodes if they tested positive for the cancer.

The doctor's assistant, Carolyn Truini, came to the exam room with her scheduling book. "I know you're a busy man with your job, so let's try to find some dates," she said. As she rattled on all the possible days, I suddenly felt a peace unlike any other in my life.

"Wait—", I interrupted her. I choked up and felt my voice crack.

"For the first time in my working life, I've got to put me first."

Carolyn smiled and nodded her approval. No doubt, she had seen countless other patients come to the same realization.

"I'll clear my calendar for Dr. Ariyan," I affirmed. "YOU tell me the date for the surgery, and I'll be there."

Soon after the initial shock of the you-have-cancer diagnosis subsided, strange things began happening to me.

I started noticing the clouds in the sky. You know those white puffy things up high in the atmosphere? They are big, and billowing, and drift overhead so softly and majestically.

I would stop and listen to the wind rustle through the leaves of the maple trees in my Connecticut yard, or the chirping crickets during the summer night through an open bedroom window.

A day's work would always follow me home into the evenings. My weekends routinely include long hours of catch-up work. I began leaving the work in the office. I would do something unheard of: relax at home at night and watch a movie. I long envied people who found the time to read books. So, I began reading books. I found the time.

I used to worry a lot. In the early 1980s, I suffered a whole year of serious anxiety. Now I could parcel out the stupid, irrelevant worries.

I started taking naps. You know, the type with a fuzzy blanket and Buddy the cat curled up against you?

I built more fires in the wood stove, and sat for long periods entranced by the flames.

I made more trips to my native Vermont. Family suddenly meant so much more.

Allen would arrange get-a-way weekends to Cape Cod without my knowledge. Rather than bitch back at him for spending the money, I treasured the escapes and how they made our love and relationship so much stronger. He didn't know which trip would be my last.

Things that used to be "major" suddenly became so darn petty: the conflicts in my boards of directors, the controversies in my local town politics, the parents screaming on TV about a teacher giving their kid a "D" instead of a "B", the fights between Democrats and Republicans, the worry about finishing all my work.

I drove slower. Drivers speeding at 80 miles per hour in a 55 limit were looking so stupid.

Calming tunes such as the *Spa* channel on satellite radio played longer inside my car. An avowed news junkie, I found myself switching off the news and opting for the solitude of silence.

I could now see the sun's rays streaming through the curtains and bouncing off the colorful quilt, whereas before all I saw was a bedroom.

Cancer is one gigantic, lovely reset button of life. Without question, I think it's the *best* side effect, a gift of the disease.

Cancer gives us an entirely new outlook on our very existence, our whole being, our purpose.

Cancer puts everything in perspective. It enables us very quickly to parcel out what really matters and what doesn't, what we value and what we don't, to appreciate being human, to express emotions we should have shown all along, to understand the fragility of life, and to value more the concept of time.

We've heard the saying, *when you've got your health, you've got everything.* Sadly, it takes the threat of a potentially terminal disease to make people realize it's really true.

When we're healthy, we take every day for granted. Our minds focus on the trivial. Cancer doesn't let us do that.

Cancer has been a big gift. My life began to change almost overnight. For patients who beat the disease, their challenge is never forgetting cancer's lesson and not returning to their old ways.

Cancer makes possible the peaceful decision to appreciate life and love more. There's a heightened awareness of everything around us.

Cancer beautifully forces us to do what we should have done all along: enjoy every minute of every hour, of every day.

Fate

THE BALDING GENE RUNS through parts of my family history. The hair on my head started thinning in earnest in my early 30s. A decade later, in my later 40s, most of my top scalp was exposed entirely.

While not a sun worshipper, I can remember a few serious episodes with sunburn in my life. The worst came during a trip to St. Croix, where just 20 minutes in the broiling Caribbean sun burned my entire body's pale Irish-American skin so bad it took two weeks to recover.

Simultaneously to all of this, mankind has been damaging the environment for at least the past 50 years. Global warming is changing the climate with more extreme weather temperatures and storms. Scientists have documented how we've impaired the ozone layer far up in the atmosphere, which screens how much ultraviolet radiation from the sun hits the Earth.

So that first day I felt the little bump atop my scalp could have easily resulted from a great confluence of events—most way out of my control, and perhaps one, the sunburn, within my control.

Was it my *fate* to get the most deadly of skin cancers, melanoma?

In the midst of my four-week hospitalization at NIH in Bethesda, I smiled broadly when the staff brought in handfuls of cards and letters. Feeling weak with hardly any immune system, they gave me a sweet shot-in-the-arm to boost my spirits.

Especially poignant among them: a note from Dr. Mary Musgrave, the head of plant science at the University of Connecticut. Together, we built up a wonderful working relationship: me, the director of our state's horticultural industries, and she, one of Connecticut's premier scientists of horticulture. She gained international acclaim for her experiments with NASA on growing plants in space aboard the space station, and as chair of the Connecticut Invasive Plants Council, among many other projects.

Just weeks after I returned home and wiggled back into a normal work schedule, a University colleague whispered to me that Mary was in the hospital. Eventually the reason came in a two-word e-mail from Mary herself: "brain tumor."

My heart sank. I reached out to her, cancer patient-to-patient. Two weeks later, she sent me a message showing the obvious effects of treatment. Despite heroic brain surgeries, radiation, and chemotherapies, Dr. Mary Musgrave died one year later, but not before I returned love and concern through constant communication and hugs. She was only 57 years old.

Was it Mary Musgrave's *fate* to get brain cancer? How ironic and sad that this eminent woman of plant science could not be saved by medical science. Yet, in contrast, that same amazing world of medical science was saving my own life. The more I thought about it, the more it confounded me.

So many cancer patients ask, "why me?" Some things we control in our lives, and some we do not. If we could look into a screen and press the "advance" button to see what will happen in our life five, ten, 20 years out from now, would we press that button? We mostly live in the present, know the past, and worry about the future. It's an elusive notion and concept—whether we call it *fate*, or *luck*, or *destiny*. Some call it *God's plan*.

Most cancer patients get their disease because it's their destiny. Some cancers can be avoided, some cannot. If you smoke two packs of cigarettes a day, you're destined to get lung cancer, right? My Dad smoked heavily, and dropped dead at age 47 of a heart attack, not cancer. So, who really knows? Did routine, everyday sun exposure to the top of my balding scalp cause my melanoma, or was it that one bad sunburn in St. Croix? I'll never know, and could drive myself crazy dwelling on it.

There are 10 trillion cells in the human body. All it takes is just one of them to cause cancer. The DNA of a single cell could corrupt prompting it to replicate wildly out of control, soon becoming cancer. Causing that could be something external, like chemicals, or cigarette smoke, or UV rays. Or it could just happen by chance, naturally.

Probably every living human being has cancerous cells in his lifetime. As NIH scientists' groundbreaking research is showing, the body's immune system sometimes reacts on its own to contain those cells, giving that person a long cancer-free life. Why it does so in your body but not mine, is both a mystery and fateful.

Can the cancer patient steer his own fate? Yes and no. Once I had the diagnosis, I decided to take command of the ship of fate by investigating all the options and choosing the best route. Treatment at Yale instead of my local hospital boosted my prospects. Opening myself to the wisdom of other patients empowered me to make daring treatment decisions. Immersing myself in the world of melanoma research opened doors to a possible cure. Choosing four major surgeries bought me more time. Landing in an NIH experimental trial (TIL adoptive cell) may have saved my life. These choices and decisions both worked against and for my fate.

The fate of cancer patients is often a numbers game. At stage three melanoma, I had a 50% likelihood of living five years. At stage four, where the cancer had traveled to my lung, my chances of dying were 95% in five years. While doctors hate giving patients those numbers, they're useful in giving us perspective in deciding how to approach our future. Knowing I had a 95% chance of dying was a pretty good incentive to go for the risky and arduous TIL treatment at NIH. My perceived bad fate pushed me to take that chance.

Death is always in our destiny. Most of us seek to extend out that fate as many years as we possibly can.

The newer science of genetic counseling may help some people avoid the fate of their ancestors, by accurately predicting they will get cancer, as did their relatives from an earlier time. We must have huge respect for those women who make the incredible decision to have elective mastectomies to avoid the breast cancer they're almost certainly destined to suffer. We're now learning that most men develop a form of relatively harmless prostate cancer in their later years, sparking a debate on whether to leave it untreated.

Timing is everything in cancer, if we want to steer our fate. I often advise patients to take treatments just because they might delay their demise long enough for the next new experimental trial to come along. I've seen that happen time and again. Go on the assumption that something effective will come along; it boosts your hope.

Along the same philosophy, a melanoma survivor with liver metastases from California gave me early precious advice: "If doctors want to cut it out, let them." If I had made that first appointment with my dermatologist one month earlier where he cut out the first lump, I might have avoided the cancer's spread. For the following four surgeries, I readily approved.

Medical science cannot yet answer why in two identical melanoma patients getting the same treatment one survives, another does not. They're getting closer as they unravel the genetic secrets hidden in cancer cells. Was it simply one person's fate that the regimen worked, while destined to fail in another? Was it difference in immune systems? The positive attitude of one over the other?

The year (1956) following my birth, singer Doris Day had a number-two hit with what would become one of my "official" cancer theme songs: *Que Sera, Sera*. Ms. Day's voice and the lyrics are ingrained in my head: "…Que sera, sera, whatever will be, will be…. the future's not ours to see…que sera, sera…. What will be, will be….".

I've sung the tune endlessly as I faced cancer. Standing in an exam room awaiting scan results, you will hear me humming it. On a gurney being wheeled into pre-op before surgery, I've hummed it—once prompting a nurse to ask if I was OK.

Cancer patients can take some consolation that their disease is controlled by fate. Fate is both beautiful and scary. When we feel control over the disease, we are more confident about our fate. I think the more confident we are, we set up ourselves for better outcomes.

Through no fault of my own, it was my fate to get melanoma. It didn't matter anyhow, because once we have cancer, we have it. Deal with it and move on. Blaming ourselves for something beyond our ability to cause is such a waste of time and energy.

None of us can control where one or two or 50 billion cancer cells travel. The human body is a miracle of plumbing and circulation. Unfortunately, that system delivers cancer to places beyond the primary site. Maybe cancer patients should sport their own bumper sticker: METASTASIS HAPPENS. When faced with it, we deal with it. We can accept the challenge with vigor.

How we master our fate is key. Perhaps if we cannot change the fate assigned to us, we can instead choose to change our attitude.

The legendary actress Ingrid Bergman died on her 67th birthday following a long bout with breast cancer. She said it best: "Cancer victims who don't accept their fate, who don't learn to live with it, will only destroy what little time they have left."

I've decided it's my fate and destiny to live. I accept that.

Knowing

On a warm Saturday, August 22, 1982, my father got up out of bed early that morning, as he always did. With Mom still sleeping, he slipped out of the house quietly to go to a second job in our hometown of New Milford, Connecticut.

Around lunchtime, he returned home. Mom could tell something wasn't quite right with him. She fixed a lunch, thinking he needed to eat after doing some physical work that morning, and that would help him.

At one point, his head went down suddenly on the dining table.

Shocked and scared, Mom suggested he go lay down in bed.

"Yeah that might help," he said.

Once in bed, he passed out again. Mom tried to arouse him. He wouldn't come to. She started to panic.

As fate would have it, at that precise moment, I decided to phone home from 300 miles away in Cape Cod where I was living at the time.

Crying uncontrollably, Mom picked up the phone. "Something's wrong with your father. I can't revive him," she sobbed into the phone to me. She was hysterical and unable to think how to summon help.

"Mom, go tend to Dad — I'm going to hang up on you and call for an ambulance," I shouted into the phone, my heart pounding.

From my location a six-hour drive away, I frantically called the local police, then nearby family and neighbors. They all rushed to the scene.

I sat anxiously by the phone in Cape Cod, waiting for news.

One hour later, the call came: "Your father didn't make it. The doctors say he died of a heart attack almost instantly."

Vincent Heffernan was 48 years old.

What if we knew we were going to die? How differently would we live our life?

What if our loved ones knew we were going to die? What would they say and do for us?

My father didn't have a clue that morning as he awoke the next few hours would be his last on this Earth.

Mom endured years of regret that she should have said special things to him, or they should have done things together. My baby brother, who was only 10 years old at the time, struggled for years with the loss of his father, as did the rest of us.

There were moments between my Dad and I in the months before his death where he was trying to break down the wall of masculinity and reach out to his oldest son about some difficulties he was having. If I had known he was going to die, I certainly would have responded a lot differently.

Without that urgency, I just shrugged him off with, "You're going to do just fine, Dad."

Very sudden illnesses or death leave so little time—or no time—to complete and finish our emotional bonds or our life's plans. There's no psychological closure. No forgiveness. As in Dad's case, there were no good-byes.

For almost all patients, cancer is a gift in that you usually have some time to prepare, to anticipate what your ending days might look like. Unlike the sudden heart attack or the sudden accident that stops a life in an instant, the cancer sufferer is receiving a precious advance warning that this *could* be the way death comes—or maybe not. Hopefully, not.

My Dad had only minutes to know he might die. I'm in year seven of my battle with cancer.

No one ever really knows how death will come. You could be diagnosed with cancer, then get hit by a car crossing the street. Or treatment might cure you, and you end up dying of old age. Today's medical science is perfecting the predictions of how a patient's disease will go. Doctors often know exactly what pain the patient will feel, thereby deliver the precise treatment for optimum patient comfort. They can often also predict with accuracy how long a patient will live.

Senator Ted Kennedy, knowing almost certainly that his brain tumor was not survivable, spent the last year of his life writing his memoir, *True Compass*. ABC News anchor Peter Jennings publicly revealed his lung cancer in April 2005, and knowing his days were numbered visited the

ABC News headquarters in June with an emotional farewell speech to staff members. Actress Farah Fawcett used her waning days to record the progress of her cancer, and the emotional good-byes with her family.

If there's one beautiful positive to come out of an ugly disease, it's that cancer gives us the ability to appreciate life's blessings, to change and become a better person, to put everything in proper perspective, and, finally, when the time comes, to arrange the most graceful and complete exit out of this life.

Just knowing that cancer might end our life spurns even the weakest psyche to rise up and show the most beautiful attributes of human nature: to draw closer in love to those matter most in our life, to get up the courage to make contact with those whom we may have shunned away, to say the things that must be said before time ends, to make amends with those wronged, and to find forgiveness in our heart for those who may have offended us.

Knowing, just knowing, we have cancer is a hidden gift.

Courage

"…he lost his courageous battle with lung cancer…"
"…she fought courageously against ovarian cancer…"
"…he waged a struggle against cancer
with courage and determination…"
"…their epic fight to beat cancer shows
their strength and courage…"

I CONFESS TO BEING a devoted reader of obituaries. They're the last published record of someone's life. But most obits leave out the cause of death. We can decipher if the person died of cancer by where the obit directs readers to send memorial contributions. The trend, however, is to point out the deceased's honorable crusade in fighting cancer to the very end.

From my earliest days as a kid getting hooked on the obituary page, I kept seeing the word *courage* or its variations over and over again. I used to wonder, what makes a person so brave in dying of cancer versus another illness?

Well, where you stand is where you sit. Today I know.

I was nervous as hell entering the dermatologist's office the day he told me I had melanoma. My fear of learning the truth about that little bump atop my scalp probably delayed my asking for the initial appointment. Imagine the courage it takes to put on a hospital gown and surgical bonnet, and feel the anxiety as you're wheeled to the operating room. Those early mornings before surgery, its takes guts just to get out of your own warm bed and make the drive to the hospital.

Courage is an internal strength, power, or determination to face a frightening challenge head-on. Cancer becomes the courage test of a lifetime. Like soldiers running into a battlefield with bullets and bombs flying, cancer patients get their training in courage in real time daily episodes in doctor's offices, hospitals, hospices, and home. They don't give us a manual or classroom exercise to learn courage.

Simply uttering the word *cancer* strikes fear in most people, mainly because the eventual outcomes are so uncertain. With polio, we take a vaccine and we're done, no fear involved. With cancer, our generations know only suffering and unpredictability. We always fear that which we can't control. We all fear what lies ahead in disease.

If a dog is chasing, we can run from the threat in fear for our life. Cancer is an internal threat from which we cannot run. We have little choice but to face it head-on, and that takes courage, knowing it is inside us.

There's no anxiety like that of a cancer patient. Anxiety signifies out-of-control fear. Nighttimes are the hardest for cancer patients. We're alone with our thoughts in the dark. Without the extra stimuli and distractions of daytime, our minds seem to race with *what ifs* about the disease. *What if it spreads? What if my insurance runs out? What if I can't handle the pain?* Many times, to regain my mental bearings, I'll force my mind to meditate on something beautiful, like the ski trail from the top of Sugarbush in Vermont, or the walk down the Old Mill dirt road next to my Connecticut home.

It takes a lot of courage just to get scan results. We patients like to call it *scanxiety*. The dread and fear can be overpowering when we wait in the exam room for the doctor to arrive. I've described the experience as crossing the line of time—on one side of the line (just before the results are given) we think you're healthy. On the other, the doctor walks in and in a split moment, he changes our life: *We found something*, or *The Cancer is gone*.

We seldom ascribe courage to our medical teams, but last time I checked they're just as human as the rest of us. Imagine we're in their shoes, and our daily job is to save clients from a horrendous enemy where sometimes they win, but far too often they lose. Nurses, oncologists, surgeons, and scientists must summon reservoirs of courage to help patients with cancer. Where do they find the strength to deliver bad news? Knowing how vital confidence is, medical professionals try valiantly to balance their intuition about where the cancer is heading against keeping patients' hopes alive.

Information can be better medicine than sedatives. The more a patient knows about his disease, the more likely he/she can muster the strength to face it. Knowledge about cancer usually empowers the patient to anticipate what lies ahead and how to handle it. Reducing fear of the unknown enables courage to take its place. Whether it's the path to a cure or learning the possibility of end of life, confidence and calm precede courage in cancer.

I think back to my Aunt Charlotte in 1980 as she was dying of liver cancer. Several times she told us heartbreakingly from her hospital bed, "I don't want to die." Yet liver cancer was nearly 100% fatal 30 years ago. We knew, and she knew, her fate was sealed. She displayed incredible courage in facing her demise, but more than that, her husband, my Uncle Larry, had to summon more fortitude in forging on to raise their five young children without her.

There's no greater courage than that of our loved ones and caregivers. We cancer patients see the fear in their faces as we lie in our treatment beds looking up at them. One woman, Agnes, comes regularly to our Yale melanoma support groups—except it's her husband who has the cancer and she needs support from the rest of us to give *her* courage to face *his* disease. We've never met him! Often our families worry more about our situation than we patients do ourselves, with good reason—their love.

How appropriate that the word *courage* derives from the French word *coeur*, meaning the *heart*. The heart powers everything in the body. Our mind is nothing without the heart, on which it depends for life and meaning. We usually connect love to our heart, but courage also makes our hearts race. Love gives us patients courage. Patients' love for our families gives them a return dose of courage.

I've come to see that courage is all about feeling fearful, but forging ahead regardless.

Faith

"Give Grandpa a kiss goodbye."

My Dad stood behind me, egging me on. I was only four years old and needed some stern coaching in my first encounter with a cancer sufferer.

Lying in the bed before me, his father was emaciated and ashen—a scary sight for this young boy. It was 1959 in Bristol, Vermont.

At age four, I quickly figured out that kiss "goodbye" would be the last one with my Grandfather Kevin Heffernan. That's a heavy lift for a little guy.

I remember the bed was low to the floor, which made it easier for my short torso to lean towards my very sick Grandpa. Using much of his remaining energy, Grandpa groaned in obvious pain as he lifted his bony body from the pillow and turned to kiss me. After he rolled back to the mattress, I stood there silently studying his face with child fascination—his horned-rim glasses and white hair forever etched in my mind. Somehow, I understood just how momentous this moment really was.

He died weeks later of stomach cancer. He was only 55 years old.

I can't get that last encounter with my Grandfather out of my mind, nor do I want to part with it. There was a holiness to that moment in time. It didn't matter that I was just four years old. Standing at that bedside, I was bestowed with the strong feeling that this man was close to God, whatever that meant, or some higher power somewhere. His wife, my beloved Gram Heffernan, would live on another 15 years, constantly holding her rosary, keeping crucifixes in every room of her Vermont home, and spraying holy water when a bad storm came.

In the days following his death, Vermont newspapers published stories revealing Grandpa's colorful past as a "fighter" in the Irish Republican Army during the Black and Tan War in 1920-1921. Officiating at his funeral in the Catholic Church were no less than *seven* priests and *five* acolytes.

In the 50+ years since his passing, I have felt that same holiness often in other cancer patients who've been part of my life. I use the term *holiness* in a broader sense. It not only means dedicated or consecrated to a God or a religious purpose, but *holiness* is also being sacred or morally and spiritually excellent.

There's something special about cancer that brings out a holiness in people, whether God-fearing or not. Call me exhibit one. Through the years of my childhood and adolescence, I gradually drifted away from the Catholic Church for many of the same reasons causing millions of American people in the baby boomer generation to become less religious than their parents and grandparents. Studies and statistics have well documented this broad secular shift away from being bound by strict religious rule.

But one little cancer cell can have a profound impact on a person's spirituality.

Strangely, after diagnosis I found myself uttering two words I hadn't said for decades: *Bless You*. They started tumbling out of my mouth that first year of treatment while chatting with one cancer patient after another. In the Yale infusion center, surrounded by others with chemo dripping into their veins, I would listen with an open heart to them talk about their lung cancer, or their ovarian cancer, or their brain cancer. "Bless you," I kept saying over and over. "Bless you." Their personal battles deserved to be consecrated.

Everybody was praying for me. All over Connecticut and Vermont there were Catholic prayers, and Jewish prayers, and Congregational prayers, and Episcopal prayers. My name was on so many prayer lists I lost track of them all. "We prayed for you at church Sunday," said a member of one of the Associations I manage, surprising me. Mass cards arrived in my home mailbox. At first, I didn't know what to say. Nobody before had ever prayed for me so openly and fervently. It was so touching and humbling that so many friends and loved ones would use the power of their personal faith to battle my disease. It also provided a powerful uplifting connection between us that proved to be another successful medical tool. Does prayer work on cancer? I'm alive and healthy in year seven despite the statistics giving me only a five per cent chance.

Cancer helped send me back to church at age 50. Allen and I decided to join a nearby Unitarian congregation full of other baby boomers travelling that same rocky road in search of spirituality and meaning to their life. Here, we could see how fellow parishioners in a chosen faith can rally around another in a time of need. Other cancer patients within the congregation would tell their story, which would be followed up with e-mails and phone calls, with visits in the hospital, help at home during treatment, and so much more. All of this becomes a wonderful psychological crutch to the cancer patient.

Faith and spirituality are two intangibles that separate humans from other animals. Evidence of it abounds in archeological diggings dating back to our earliest ancestors. So long as we are human and alive, we feel some sort of faith or spiritual feeling, regardless of whether we are religious, agnostic, or atheistic. It is human, it is who we are, and it is beautiful. What I may believe is different somehow from what you believe. We each have our freedom to think, to pursue what inspires us, and no one can take that away from us.

Cancer patients often are not aware of their true power of faith until the stress and fear of their disease hits them head-on. We're so busy leading our daily lives that faith and spirituality sometimes hides deep in our minds, placed and stored there for activation when needed.

"The wise man in the storm prays God, not for safety from danger, but for deliverance from fear," said author Ralph Waldo Emerson. Whatever your faith, it's a great tool to set aside and manage fear of cancer, which no patient ever fully escapes.

One friend told me the story of her father who had gone into a coma from advanced cancer, where he had been mumbling the names of his dead brothers and boyhood friends. One day he awoke from the coma. "We heard you talk about Frank and Tony while you were sleeping," she told her father. "Oh yeah," her Dad shot back, "they said 'go back, it's not your time'." He lived a good life with the cancer for several more years. Stories like this only confirm the power of belief.

Faith sometimes is that lynchpin in the mind-body connection. For some, just believing a higher power, like God, will beat back their disease is enough to trigger a remission. For others, faith and spirituality provide a calming confidence, and a power and determination that directs the body to fight the cancer, or at least manage symptoms more easily. I had absolute faith that science and research would help me whip cancer's ass, and so far it has. But the important point is, *I had to believe in it heart and soul*. I had to have faith.

Most cancer patients turn to the God they worship. Others find faith in the people they love, perhaps in their medical team, maybe an Angel who watches over them. Some see their spirituality in the beauty of life around them, or the power of their own minds, body, and existence. Regardless of the origin, it becomes the strength of soul and purpose that sustains the cancer patient. We probably see this in people suffering other diseases, but at this stage of human history, it is most prominent with cancer.

I think this explains why we remember crystal-clear every word, every action of cancer patients who have touched our lives, and our precious moments with them. Their struggle, their joy, their experience become holy and honorable. We become enriched and blessed.

Campaigns

THE BODY NEEDS A good week to recover strength from Interleukin-2 treatment.

In October 2009, Yale hospitalized me the second and fourth weeks for as many intravenous doses of IL-2 as I could endure. It was the last FDA-approved regimen for my melanoma with a success rate of only 6%.

I dreaded going through this treatment that ramped up my immune system so much it began attacking my skin. My body swelled with 20 pounds of liquid retention. It made me nauseous, sickly, sleepless, and I was in constant danger of too-low blood pressure from capillary leakage.

But here was my motivation and strategy: even though I expected the $285,000 IL-2 medication wouldn't work (tests weeks later showed the tumors kept growing), the treatment was a prerequisite for the TIL adoptive cell procedure at NIH in Bethesda. I had to go through IL-2—and it had to fail—in order for me to be considered for the primo TIL treatment. As a cancer patient, I had done my due diligence. TIL became my focus and target therapy.

Yale finally discharged me the last Saturday morning of October, sending me home exhausted and looking like I had some sort of plague.

On my calendar just four days later, the first week of

November 2009, I had signed up months earlier to be a patient advocate at a huge translational research conference in Tysons Corner, Virginia organized by—most importantly— the National Cancer Institute of NIH, the same institution that would decide whether TIL could be performed on my melanoma.

"You sure you feel up to going?," my husband Allen asked me.

"I'll be OK. I've *got* to do this!", I insisted.

Some 800 cancer specialists, scientists, and researchers from around the country would be there, sharing results of their trials and experiments. The task for us 30 patient advocates was to inject the patient perspective as to how the science could be translated into action at the clinical level for cancer sufferers. Yale had nominated me to go.

Most critical in my mind: the conference named me to co-chair a session on melanoma and adoptive cell science with Dr. Patrick Hwu, a prominent physician and researcher who had worked with the TIL pioneer at NIH, Dr. Steve Rosenberg. Hwu had moved from NIH to start a TIL program at M.D. Anderson Cancer Center in Houston.

There was no way I could miss the conference. Allen drove the car for me on the 325-mile trek down from Connecticut that Tuesday night. Walking from the hotel registration to our room, I felt light-headed. For the first time in my life, I asked Allen if we could order dinner by room service, thinking I didn't have the energy to walk to a restaurant.

The next morning, just after the opening general session, I felt so weak I returned to our room for an hour's nap. But as the day wore on, my stamina slowly returned. By Thursday,

I mapped out some 20 stops at melanoma-related projects being displayed on poster boards around the hotel by those scientists, their faces showing surprise at talking directly with a stage four melanoma patient. Each of those contacts might be the next breakthrough in curing my cancer.

I threw myself into the campaign for Bob. Like politicians running for office, I had declared my candidacy for a second term of life. This campaign would last several years.

The world of cancer is full of campaigns, both personal crusades like my own and public operations, elaborate and localized, to offset the disease.

I was no stranger to campaigns. Those seven years I served on the U.S. Senate staff exposed me to campaigns for election and reelection, to campaigns for approving nominations, and to campaigns to pass bills. I simply applied the campaign models I knew to the latest serious challenge in my life, melanoma.

Cancer cries out for a campaign. There's a critical need, a terrible threat, and a search for the answer or solution. Campaigns involve people, sometimes lots of people. Campaigns find the precise pressure point, and then apply that pressure. Campaigns are all about making connections and finding resources.

The campaign for Bob had clear objectives: find the best treatment, hospital, and doctors, and help other patients simultaneously. That's why I could not miss the NCI/NIH conference, even though my weakened health coming out of IL-2 just days earlier should have kept me at home. The meeting connected me to the nation's best experts. I brought home insight to share with fellow patients. Hopefully, the scientists came away with new perspectives from my experience. The more fellow patients, medical professionals, researchers, and scientists I involved in my personal campaign to lick cancer, the better the chance that I would have a good outcome, both medically and spiritually.

We can sit at home and cry about our cancer, or we can roll up our sleeves and dive into the public world of cancer. We can isolate ourself or we can help others. I strongly believe that when patients decide to regard their assault on their cancer as a campaign, they reap the double benefit of connecting themselves to the best, the brightest and the latest advances, AND improving the plight of others.

People everywhere are campaigning to fight cancer. Millions of people get galvanized each year to march in walks, engage in fundraisers, spread messages via the media, connect in web-based social portals like Facebook, and more. This brutal disease motivates family and friends to do things they never anticipated. They're turning their grief and concern into action.

Celebrities like Lance Armstrong use their fame to bring campaigns alive for cancers previously below radar, such as his testicular cancer. TV news anchor Katie Couric triggered intrigue nationwide when televising her colonoscopy, fighting the colon cancer that took the life of her husband.

Allen and I walk in the Swim Across the Sound fundraiser that helps the cancer center at St. Vincent's Hospital in Bridgeport, Connecticut, where he works. Bike rides like the *CT Challenge* and Yale's *Closer to Free* bike-a-thon inspire thousands to donate and become involved. There's the American Cancer Society's *Relay for Life*, Susan G. Komen's *Race for the Cure*, and melanoma's *Outrun the Sun* race or *Hope on the Slopes* fundraisers at ski areas. Rather than fading in popularity, the challenge of these campaigns spur more excitement, especially when they are close to a cancer patient.

Campaigns surrounding cancer take the form of advocacy. Melanoma advocates nationwide are convincing state legislatures to adopt new laws banning indoor tanning for kids under age 18. Not only will the campaign raise awareness of how dangerous excessive tanning is, and how the cure for melanoma is far off, it also brings a behind-the-scenes cancer to the public forefront. The American Lung Association fights for cleaner air laws and regulations.

Hope and science alone will not end cancer. Human sheer will and determination, the banding together of the afflicted and their loved ones, and the voices of advocacy will round out the total force for healing and wellness. Campaigns surrounding cancer give that lift of energy and resources to fuel hope and science.

Legacy

I**F YOU DIED TOMORROW**, would you have left a mark in this life?

Most of us want to endow this planet a little piece of us for posterity. We'd like to leave the Earth in better shape than we found it. It's basic human nature to want to fix and improve things, to advance the world and enhance the future for all mankind.

We think of our kids, and their kids. We wonder about future generations. If we can save them from future pain and suffering, we are determined to do it. If we can make their lives easier through technological advances, we will invest in it. We will invent it.

We want desperately to think that our lives had meaning and value. That we really accomplished something. That we had some sort of an impact in this life, maybe on society, perhaps on human systems, certainly on the people who were part of our lives.

Most of us want to leave a *legacy* that we are proud of—especially cancer patients.

⸎   ⸏

As a young man in my early 20s, some 30 years before cancer would strike, I could feel the legacy thing encompass me. Serving on the staff of the United States Senate in Washington from 1974-1981, I could see legacies being created all around me, every day. They took the form of enacting laws that would serve American citizens by the millions for many years.

Several amazing twists of fate and circumstance placed me at the center of the three-year legislative drive to establish the U.S. Department of Education. I couldn't help but be overwhelmed with a legacy-in-the-making when I stood in the East Room of the White House as the President finally signed into law the bill that had consumed my personal energy night-and-day for three years.

There exists today a Cabinet department of the federal government, a Secretary of Education in the President's Cabinet that will impact hundreds of millions of citizens as they pursue education and lifelong learning. I had a hand in making that happen.

And as if that wasn't enough, I would spend the next year writing a book telling the story of how the new agency was born, titled *Cabinetmakers*.

Now, those are two monumental legacies that I bestow unto others. But, as tremendous as they are, they pale in comparison to the opportunities cancer gave me.

A beautiful byproduct of cancer is that the disease enables us to fashion a legacy.

Whether they know it or not, even those simple-lived cancer patients who simply showed up for treatment and went home contributed to science's understanding of the illness. Figures are compiled daily about patients' treatments and outcomes. The sheer volume of this data gives oncologists a macro view of progress and priorities. We leave a legacy, just by being a cancer patient.

I recently counseled a melanoma buddy, Brad: "you had an impact on science, and you can be proud of that." I had pushed to get Brad admitted to the TIL adoptive cell treatment at NIH, where he arrived with advanced stage four tumors, but he was a perfect, young candidate for the protocol. Everything was moving on-track for him when sadly, just an hour before doctors would begin taking down his immune system, word came from the NIH lab that his new TIL cells mysteriously stopped growing and were dying off in cell culture dishes. Emotionally, the sudden news was devastating. NIH had no choice but to send him back home to his doctors in South Carolina. Months later, he would fight for his life as the cancer entered his brain. But this is for certain: Brad's experience will figure in the body of research into this treatment. Scientists will learn from him. His is a quieter legacy that thousands of cancer patients bequeath to the rest of us every day.

Contrast Brad's legacy with that of another cancer patient, Steve Jobs, the founder of Apple Computer. His work and inventions have changed the lives of *billions* of people around the globe. Yet, Jobs knew that his pancreatic cancer—mostly fatal for the majority of patients—only emboldened himself to work harder in the time he had left to perfect that precious legacy. At a famous graduation speech he gave, Jobs said, "Remembering that I'll be dead soon is the most important tool I've ever encountered to help me make the big choices in life. Because almost everything—all external expectations, all pride, all fear of embarrassment or failure—these things just fall away in the face of death, leaving only what is truly important. Remembering that you are going to die is the best way I know to avoid the trap of thinking you have something to lose. You are already naked. There is no reason not to follow your heart."

For most patients, cancer gives us some time to plan out and produce that legacy. It could be leaving part of our estate to a nonprofit organization that deals with cancer. It could be mentoring other patients dealing with the same disease. It could be participating in a trial for a new drug, or giving up our cancer cells for research.

Sometimes, the love for a cancer patient spurs others to create that lasting legacy, either during the patient's life or after he/she's gone. Two years after Susan Komen died of breast cancer at age 36, her younger sister established in 1982 the Susan G. Komen Breast Cancer Foundation, which has raised over $2 billion for medical research, education, advocacy, and health services.

My cancer legacy is one of giving back. I told Yale scientists to take and work with my cancer cells long before they had the chance to ask me. I insisted that medical students be part of my medical team, hoping that at least one of them would be inspired by this melanoma patient to concentrate in this discipline. I chose to place myself in a difficult, groundbreaking trial 300 miles from home at NIH that could change how cancer is treated. I served as a patient advocate to advise researchers. I worked to improve Yale-New Haven Hospital on a patient/family centered care council. This book is a documented, inspirational tool to help others for years to come.

How we exit anything in life speaks volumes about our personal character. How we leave a job, how we end a relationship, how we whip cancer's ass, and of course, how we die.

We've all seen the "bad" exits in life. The American President who had to resign in disgrace. The talented movie star caught up in drug abuse. The winning football coach exposed as a pedophile. These are exits that negated what otherwise should have been remarkable legacies.

But for cancer patients, it's different. The disease chose us, not the other way around. Like the celebrities mentioned above, cancer patients naturally draw others into their lives, into their experience in fighting the disease. Without even trying, cancer survivors are handed legacy-making capabilities. People will remember that five-mile walk we did to raise funds for cancer research. They'll pause in amazement at the thought of our courage in absorbing each treatment. They're so impressed that we went public with our cancer. They'll remember the things we said to them as we approached end of life.

We don't have to die to leave a legacy. I'm expecting to live a long life, and still leave a legacy from my experience with melanoma. More than that, I expect to live another 30+ years, and who knows how many other legacies I'll create.

What's going to be your legacy?

Take Steve Jobs advice: to create your own legacy, all you really have to do is simply *follow your heart*.

Hugs

AT THE END OF our melanoma support group meeting at Yale in August 2009, our patients and families were still talking out in the hallway.

I looked over at Lee Banks and impulsively stretched open my arms. "Lee, give me a big hug, please," I insisted. The two of us embraced strongly as his wife Ruth looked on. From one stage four cancer patient to another, it was a powerful emotional moment, a bond like no other on Earth. A soccer athlete in his middle age, Lee's muscles radiated warmth and appreciation deep into my soul.

I worried it could be one of my last moments with Lee. My intuition was right. He died three months later on Thanksgiving Day with melanoma metastases in his brain and elsewhere. I never saw him again.

But that one hug gave both of us strength and hope— intimately and exclusively human emotions. And I'll never forget it.

Unlike some cultures in Europe and other countries, Americans seem to have these norms of detachment that prevent PDAs—public displays of affection. I have to confess that I myself fell victim to it. Looking back pre-cancer, I recall I reserved hugging solely for close family members. Everyone else would get a handshake.

Today, it makes big news when a person stands on the street and holds up a sign offering "FREE HUGS". TV cameras rush to the scene because it's so odd. But, you know, that makes us smile. Nobody calls for the hugger to be imprisoned or whisked away to a mental hospital. Secretly, we all wish we could be just like that—open arms and loving.

The American medical and legal establishments particularly frown upon body-to-body contact. Priests and pastors—the very people chosen to convey God's love—are sued left and right for alleged abuses and molestation claims. More physicians bring an assistant into the patient's exam room to bear witness that everything is on the up-and-up. Malpractice insurance premiums rise higher based on the liability of the inappropriate *touch*.

What on earth have we done to ourselves? The beauty and innocence of a simple hug between two people is powerful and beneficial. Thankfully, science can document this. A 2003 study by psychologist Karen Grewen with the School of Medicine at the University of North Carolina-Chapel Hill revealed blood pressure soared in no-contact people versus the huggers in the study. Their systolic (upper) reading jumped 24 points, more than double the rise for huggers, and their diastolic (lower) also rose significantly higher. Heart rate increased 10 beats a minute for those without contact compared with five beats a minute for huggers.

I've discovered cancer patients have a special license to hug more often, and to hug others beyond their friends and lovers.

Screw the many norms of masculine detachment, I decided soon after my cancer diagnosis. I may not be on this planet much longer, so I'm going to be a real human being. If I want to hug someone, they're getting a hug. Hear this: *nobody* has ever refused my hug.

How wonderful that many of my Yale medical team routinely gives hugs (probably horrifying the Yale legal staff). I give hugs to the receptionists in the Yale clinic. I reached out and received a big impromptu hug from NIH Dr. Jenny Hong when she told me my TIL procedure was finished so I could go home. NIH Dr. Mark Dudley got an emotional hug from me upon seeing my new TIL cells in his lab. There are hugs for fellow patients, hugs for coworkers, hugs for crusaders, and hugs for Dr. Ruth and her scientists working on my melanoma cell line at Yale.

My final hug with Lee Banks taught me how precious and unforgettable such an embrace can be. And yes, it was a power hug between *two men*. When you hug someone, you feel an inner surge of touch and warmth. The shoulders meet, the chests press together, and the arms wrap around each other.

Hugs are universal across all cultures, but the fact that we Americans do less of it actually makes a hug delivered more powerful. The best hugs are the ones where the embrace lasts several seconds longer, and the two bodies rock a little from side to side, and the hands pat the backs.

Cancer enables people to let down their guard and show

some true, spontaneous emotion. My hugs are healing, calming, reassuring. My hugs convey the highest gratitude, love, and appreciation. My hug says, feel me for I am alive. Treasure and remember this moment we connected.

Cure

Every cancer patient aspires to hear the words: *You're cured*.

From the very moment we're diagnosed, we want to be rid of the disease. That's the ultimate goal. We want doctors and treatments to zap every last cancer cell. Cut it out, drug it out, nuke it out. Cancer be gone, and never come back again! Every treatment decision I ever made had that simple objective in my sights: to be *cured*.

We're united in this zeal for a *cure* with our families, our medical teams, and the entire society that surrounds us. All of the emotional energy, the research, the financial resources, the medical industrial complex, nonprofit cancer advocacy organizations, and the public policies that support us cancer survivors are built around pursuit of—the *cure*.

BUT, the "c" word — *cure* — is rarely or cautiously used by most medical doctors, because they can never know for certain that all the cancer cells are truly gone. Melanoma patients experience recurrences sometimes 5, 10, 15 years later.

In six years of my treatment, not once has any of the dozens of medical professionals who cared for me uttered the word *cure* to me. We push them to tell us which treatment will cure us. We can't rest until we hear them officially pronounce that we're cured. Yet they shy away from saying it.

The amazing thing is doctors' and nurses' own desire to attain a *cure* in their patients is what drives them every day to work so hard. The very word they can't say is the great motivator that frames their career.

Cure is almost too absolute a medical term. The published literature is riddled with predictions that the cure to cancer was at hand, or attainable with the revelation of a new medical discovery. When President Nixon launched America's "war on cancer" in 1971, a cure for cancer seemed as possible as President Kennedy's pledge to land on the moon. An April 2013 cover story of *Time* magazine boldly proclaims, *How To Cure Cancer*. Forty-two years after that war-on-cancer presidential declaration, we're much closer to understanding cancer, yet cures remain elusive for many sufferers. Progress has not been consistent among cancers; for some survival rates have drastically improved, but not for others.

So, the world of oncology over time developed its own lexicon for *cure*, and we patients have grudgingly gone along:

- Instead of being *cured*, you're in *remission*, where the cancer appears to be gone but, who knows, it could come back
- When tumors appear to be retreating, thereby raising hopes of a cure in the patient's mind, the treatment is eliciting a *partial response*

- The disappearance of the cancer within a fairly short period of time from treatment is called a *complete response* or is *NED*—no evidence of disease.
- And most gratifying of all, when a longer period of time has passed with no sign of the cancer, the patient is in a *durable remission*.

Perhaps we cancer survivors should develop our own interpretation of *cure*.

What constitutes a *cure* to us obviously can differ from our doctor. That age-old disconnect stubbornly persists even as medicine advances to allow more survivors to live longer. I think it's good if doctors and patients can have a discussion about each's views of *cure*.

Maybe we survivors could just drop our sights and expectations a little. I may not be *cured*, but by gosh living a wonderful three years of healthy life with no new melanoma is as good as a cure in my mind. I considered myself cured of nausea five weeks after the TIL adoptive cell treatment, but that scourge can revisit me anytime. Time and healing finally cured the sharp, intense pain when NIH surgically removed a tumor to harvest my TIL cells.

Maybe oncologists are correct: we demand a lot out of the word *cure*. But it's a term, a state of being, the dream, desire and hope to move on in our lives without cancer. Or, at least manage the cancer to the point that it's a minor imposition in daily existence.

There's not a more powerful exhilaration in life than to think or know you've whipped cancer. Or that somehow you've contributed to finding cures.

Dr. Rosenberg in his book *The Transformed Cell* beautifully describes how even those patients who surmised they might not survive cancer were eager to enter one of his NIH trials so they might help scientists find an answer to help people long after they passed on. Such a treasured, unselfish gift to humanity!

Often we've talked about finding *the cure* for cancer. There may never be a single cure. Instead, today's science tells us to expect varieties of cures. The immune system may hold the answer for melanoma, but not for brain cancer. Genetic therapies like Vemurafenib targeting the BRAF mutation may work only temporarily to knock down the cancer until those cells mutate again to outfox the treatment. We may be entering an era of scientific research leading us to customizing therapies for each person, instead of the old system of this-chemo-works-for-all.

What price should we expect to pay for a cure? Or for an effective treatment that attacks the cancer long enough and well enough so we can continue to enjoy our lives? Costing out cancer care is one of our thorniest issues. Will the people of America get a good return on their million-dollar-plus investment in my treatment to keep me alive? How do we even consider the value of preserving a human life against the outrageous cost to develop a new treatment? As a nation, we decided 40 years ago that we cannot rely solely on the profit motives of private industry to find cures; the nonprofit work of universities, hospitals, advocacy groups, and the

National Cancer Institute of NIH is critical to making new discoveries.

If I told you there is a cure for your cancer, but it's too expensive, what would you think? What would you do? How angry would you get? The TIL adoptive cell treatment that hopefully, maybe has cured me is a prime example. Hospitals like Yale think it's too expensive without insurance reimbursement. That's why only two U.S. and one Israeli facility other than NIH have dared to start up a lab to grow the TIL cells.

Wrapped up in ventures to find cancer cures are these momentous, mind-numbing cost-benefit quandaries with no easy answers. The bad news is financial limitations may thwart discovery. The good news is that's overpowered by a common, unified human determination to beat cancer, to find *cures*.

⁓ ⁓

Cure was definitely on my mind a crisp, cool late November day 2012 at Union Station in downtown New Haven, Connecticut.

Along with my oncologist Harriet Kluger and some 20 other Yale doctors, nurses, and survivors of many cancers, we were filming Yale's new, ambitious promotional campaign centered around a very simple concept—*Closer to Free*.

Yale's marketing team had assembled over 70 more dancers, singers, and survivor families for an uplifting flash mob—all singing and dancing to Smilow Cancer Hospital's theme song, *Closer to Free*. The event would produce several TV spots to air first during the Super Bowl, and often throughout the year. I was one of six patients holding up a survivor sign whilst the roar of joyous signing and dancing and clapping celebrated all around me. You can't watch it without getting choked up.

We want to be cured of cancer. Until we reach that beautiful goal, we strive every day to get closer and closer to being healthy and happy. We want to be free of pain, free of worry, free of heartbreak, free of daily sickness, and free of cancer. The human journey of getting there brings out the beauty in all of us.

Listen, as we all sing together…

Everybody wants to live how they want to live
Everybody needs a chance once in a while
Everybody wants to love how they want to love
Everybody wants to be closer to free
Closer to free! Yeah! Closer to free…..

Hope

"THERE'S ALWAYS HOPE."

One of our fellow Yale melanoma patients and his wife sat in the exam room with their oncologist. He had come to the end of his rope. He had all the immune-based treatments and nothing worked. There were now multiple melanoma tumors in his brain. Several surgeries and gamma-knife radiation shots did little to halt the cancer's advance.

Together, they sat there in one of the world's foremost bastions of medicine—Yale-New Haven—and together, patient, spouse and doctor, they arrived at that moment where there was nothing more medicine could do.

After a long pause, with the air thick with doom, their Doctor softly assured them, "There's always hope." That moment comforted them greatly.

Hope is one of the permanent treatment options for cancer. It's not covered by insurance. It costs nothing. Hopes lives in the free human spirit.

Many times I heard my beloved Dr. Harriet Kluger tell me, "Let's hope for the best." Beginning that first awful year of Interferon, my good doctor told me, "Let's hope it works", although both of us knew the chances were small it would.

Harriet was hopeful my first lung surgery at Yale would retrieve the metastases and that would be the end of it.

My Yale medical teams beautifully mixed hope with science. They understood my emotional wishes for a cure were key to whether their whole treatment plan became successful. At NIH, the institution steeped purely in science, I heard the word "hope" only from chaplains. Yet I'm quite certain at a personal level, the NIH staff was *hoping* their experiments and research would beat cancer. Even the most geeky research scientists harbor hopes and dreams that motivate them to press on in spite of repeated failures.

Doctors often say there's always hope because they know a new treatment or cure could come at any time. The advances and findings of scientists into new genetic pathways, for example, give them encouragement that a new drug could soon arise. Hope is tied to time and timing. I had a close relative who died of HIV in 1987—if only he could have lived a few more months and years, his life might have been saved. We hoped for effective treatments, and they came.

Hope sometimes is the best medicine. An old Irish proverb says, *Hope is the physician of each misery.*

Hope is the desire and belief that, somehow, somewhere, a good result is ahead in our future. Hope is a uniquely powerful human emotion. I think it's tied intimately to the positive side of all of us. Our hope and our optimism are inseparable.

Whether they know it or feel it or not, there is hope in every cancer patient. Hope is prevalent because the disease's course is so unpredictable and high-risk. With appendicitis, surgeons remove the appendix and send the patient home to recover; problem solved. With cancer, stray cells can linger to cause more distress years ahead. Hope becomes so much more imperative with cancer.

Hope also marches forward with confidence. For some unknown reason, I always seemed to have the confidence that *something* would eventually work on my cancer. Despair—the opposite human emotion—would drag me down each time I got bad scans or the news that a treatment failed, or the tumors grew rather than shrunk. But those hopeful feelings always lifted me back up to face whatever came next.

Only a few months into my first treatments, I found myself signing e-mails and letters with the closing, *Love and Hope, Bob*. I still do it to this day.

Psychologists believe hope comes when there is a goal in mind. For a cancer patient, the ultimate goal is *cure*. We hope that our treatments cure us. But we also have other goals, such as living long enough to see a child get married or a child to be born. Perhaps another goal is simply to be comfortable, or to feel no side effect. We hope that medicine makes us feel better.

It's hard to know which comes first: hope or willpower. To have hope of beating cancer, I had to have the will to live. I also needed strength and determination. Hope arises when we are faced with a crisis or a tough challenge. Lottery players hope they win despite 100 million-to-One odds against them. I was determined to win my battle against stage four melanoma despite the 95% mortality rate.

Hope is not a patient-exclusive feeling; it's forceful

in those who care about and love us. Hope and love are often intertwined. I've seen it so many times in families who refuse to take *no* for an answer and search out new treatments for their loved ones. One young daughter in her 20s from Dallas, Texas contacted me after reading my TIL adoptive cell story, hoping the same treatment would help her mother with melanoma brain mets. Their doctor said flatly the mother would die, but the daughter would not give up hope, and continued searching the world for another solution.

A landscaper from eastern Connecticut who once presided on the Board of an association I manage surprised me to tears one day when he asked if he could talk to me privately. In his hands, he held a paper bag. "I've been working on this," he said as he reached inside, "hope you like it. Your struggle really inspired me." He pulled out a thick 6-inch by 9-inch slab of white marble quarried from my home state of Vermont. He had spent many long hours chiseling the letters H O P E into both sides of the rock. I cherish that gift.

Hope and determination can move mountains, change the world, and beat back cancer.

Nobody displays this power more than Nelson Mandela, the South African man who proudly campaigned all his life to end apartheid, was thrown in jail for 27 years because of it, and rose from the depths of despair to become his nation's first popularly-elected President and win the Nobel Peace Prize.

So many cancer patients are Nelson Mandelas. Time

and again, they climb from the deepest valleys to the highest mountains. Their own personal struggles are equally as honorable.

Life

SOMETIMES IT TAKES A jolt like cancer to force a new appreciation for life and living.

From our first breaths at birth, we dwell on the moment's challenges and pleasures. As we grow from children to adolescents to adults, we become consumed by the routines of hitting the alarm clock, showering, breakfasting, commuting, working, lunching, commuting, dining, TV, reading, arguing, conspiring, strategizing, tiring, sleeping.... and the cycle repeats day after day. If we look into the future, typically it's worrying about money to pay the bills, the kids misbehaving, the conflicts at work, our personal relationships, or the material stuff malfunctioning or ready to break down.

Unless we suffer from hypochondria, we rarely give our health much thought unless and until something goes wrong. And even then, we tend to blow up little maladies out of proportion: that itchy skin we can't stand any more, or the headache preventing us from thinking straight, or the annoying heartburn.

We're prone to take life, with all its true meaning and glory, for granted—until it's threatened, truly threatened. Among all people, cancer is the universal threat to life.

I used to think the big losses in my life had taught

me enduring lessons about the value of living—the sudden death of my father at the top of the list. Honestly, they served more as *temporary* reminders of life's fragility. Once the shock eventually wore off, the mind-numbing routine of daily life would return.

But having cancer inside your body is so much more different and life changing. From the moment I stepped outdoors from Dr. Godwin's fateful pronouncement, "This came back as a malignant melanoma", all my mind's focus was on life and living. And it's never left me since.

The value that a cancer patient affixes to life always goes up after diagnosis. Cancer diverts our attention away from the mundane to what's really important. Cancer has the power to change our previous notions about life, or at least prompt a major reassessment. Cancer may force our habits to change. Cancer will likely encourage us to appreciate love and people in your life. Cancer will slow us down to savor life.

Hundreds of books and movies tell lovely stories of cancer patients doing things they probably otherwise never would have done. Who could forget the 2007 film *The Bucket List* about two terminally ill men escaping from a cancer ward and heading off on a road trip with a wish list of to-dos before they died? My melanoma buddy Mark Driggs, suffering from brain mets, parachuted out of an airplane recently. "Another item crossed off my bucket list," he said gleefully in an e-mail to us fellow patients.

Like most people, I was too busy living the rat race to dwell much on the meaning of life. So long as I could get a good night's sleep, manage well on the income I earned, and avoid too much stress, I was quite happy. I was always living in the moment.

But melanoma compelled me to look at details closer. Looming larger in front of my face was life I hadn't seen before. I still wanted to swat that fly buzzing around my head, but suddenly I realized it had a life on this planet just as I had, and what right did I have to end the life of something living—especially since I was desperately fighting to save my own life. I used to think a university scientist I knew personally was eccentric because he caught insects inside the house and released them unharmed outdoors. Now with cancer, I can understand.

I used to mow over the crickets in the lawn; now I let them pass unharmed.

Driving down the highway, hitting a squirrel with the car became an emotionally sad ordeal for me. The other night, I braked hard to avoid a raccoon, another wild, beautiful, innocent animal just living his life. My heart sank at the bump-bump sound under the car.

I put off the necessary decision to end the life of a majestic maple tree in my front yard, beset by a disease that made it a danger to fall on the house. Ten years ago, I wouldn't have given it much thought, but that tree held memories that bonded with me—we both grew up together. A life shared together.

Cancer made me ultra-sensitive to suffering. Whether animal or human, I now can appreciate that avoiding suffering and pain is critical to enjoying life and living.

Life's relationships to loved ones and friends take on greater meaning post-cancer. I made more time for them. I expressed more love. I valued them as never before. Being alive is human and emotional.

Simpler things became more beautiful and enjoyable—the hot shower, falling asleep on the couch, the wind rustling through the leaves in the backyard, a walk down the dirt road. Life is not about money and material things. It's about breathing, seeing, hearing, loving, and enjoying the littlest things.

As cancer survivors, we may start wondering, what have we missed in this life? But we can't change the past. We have to focus on our future and enjoying every day of our life.

If a cancer treatment could save your life, how much would you pay for it?

Or maybe the better question is: how much would your insurance company pay? Or, at what point does society or the medical establishment deem a treatment worthy of the cost? When is that treatment considered too expensive, regardless of how many lives it could save?

We know the emotional, moral, physical, and spiritual value of life is *priceless*. Yet every day life-and-death decisions are based on treatment cost. My good Doctor Kluger once remarked that for some patients, she spent more time getting cost approval than actually treating that patient.

I've been personally drawn into the ethical and moral quandary of costly medical procedures versus outcomes by the very treatment that saved my life: TIL adoptive cell therapy pioneered at NIH. About one-third of all TIL patients see their melanoma eliminated, yet after nearly 30 years of work at NIH only two other American hospitals are offering it. Why? "It's too expensive," a Yale official told me.

In reality, TIL is not any more expensive than bone marrow transplants for leukemia. But because TIL is not yet FDA-approved, nor covered by insurance companies, the U.S. medical establishment considers it *exotic* at the moment—despite that fact that no other treatment has a higher success rate for stage four melanoma.

So, at what point does preservation of life trump the cost?

Regardless of these tough issues, all of modern medicine is built around the conviction that life is to be saved. Trillions of dollars' worth of buildings and equipment bear witness to this. Millions of medical staff report to work each day in the fervent hope of saving lives. Millions more patients and families expect and depend on that common love of life. We know they're there to treat us, make us feel better, and above all else, do whatever they can to save our precious lives.

One of my favorite authors, Dr. Rachel Naomi Remen, wrote in her book *My Grandfather's Blessings:* "The capacity to bless life is in everybody. The power of our blessing is not diminished by illness or age."

With cancer, I began to see the commonality of life. All of us actually have more traits and feelings in common than we realize. We agree more than we disagree, but it might take a life-threat to reveal that.

The debate over abortion exposes this clearly. Both pro-lifers and pro-choicers alike agree on the importance of life. Both also want healthy and loved children. And

I'm hopeful both sides can agree on preventing unwanted pregnancies, which makes abortion unnecessary. For such a critical issue concerning life, they have more in common than they realize.

I love how cancer brings together people of disparate belief systems. The battle unites them in ways they never thought possible. I once shared tears and got a sweet hug from a macho "fag-hating" man (his words) man during cancer treatment together. The disease beautifully breaks down stupid barriers to reveal we're all human and in this life together.

The will to live is common to both believers in God and in atheists or agnostics. Virtually all faiths emphasize the sanctity of human life. I've experienced religious services in at least 10 different faiths, and appreciation for life is a common thread that runs through them. The concept of heaven extends our concept of life beyond death, because we treasure life so much. Conversely, my discussions with atheists and agnostics show they value life just as highly because, in their words, since they don't believe in an afterlife their current existence is all they have, so it becomes precious and priceless.

Whether God-loving or god-less, most cancer patients love life and choose to fight cancer with all the inner strength they can muster.

So, here's to life, to love, to joy. Here's to all the cancer survivors and warriors. Here's to their loved ones. Here's to hope that science and medicine will one day make ordeals like mine a mere nuisance. Here's to *you*.

Epilogue

"EVERY TIME I COME into this room, it's been the same result," smiled Dr. Jim Yang, the veteran NIH medical doctor and scientist, during one of my routine check-ups in Bethesda.

I'm still an active research subject. Return visits to NIH went from monthly, to every two months, then every three months, then four months, and now six-month intervals.

I have passed the three-year mark out from my TIL adoptive cell treatment. For three years straight, the CT scans continue to show two tiny "spots" in my right lung. They either reduced slightly in size, or they remained stable since the experimental therapy in February-March 2010. Brain scans stayed clear. Thankfully, no new cancer anywhere else.

To my Yale doctors, those spots could be dead tumors showing as scar tissue. To the NIH doctors, I will not be considered in a *durable remission* until the spots vanish completely off the scans. All my doctors agreed this is the most unpredictable cancer—melanoma could roar back at any time, surprising no one.

"No you can't remove the bracelets!," Dr. Yang admonished me. I was tiring of the clunky chains on my left wrist that say *irradiated blood only* and *no steroids unless medical emergency.* "We've got to protect your new cells. They're still working for you. They could be containing active metastases," he insisted.

About the visible only side effect from the TIL treatment are white spots scattered in my skin, called vitiligo. My new TIL cells may be confusing skin cells for melanoma cells. I point to those white spots with honor, as evidence NIH's cell engineering is performing well.

How differently would I have written this book if my experience had turned the way statistics predict for stage four melanoma: a 95% mortality rate in five years?

If you have gotten this far in the book, you know by now that I've been through a lot of pain, suffering, heartbreak, and doom. My body looks like knives have attacked me. My joints ache, and my energy has never returned to pre-cancer levels.

I've also personally met over 300 other cancer survivors since I was diagnosed. I've seen several lose their battle. I've joined the Yale-Smilow Cancer Hospital patient advisory council hoping to make a difference. I've been loyal to Yale's melanoma support group, helping others cope. I've posted my story on five major websites, resulting in almost daily contacts from melanoma sufferers across the globe. I take seriously my role as a patient advocate for Yale's melanoma research program.

My spirit of perseverance and hope has never wavered. Not once. Maybe it's just who I am. But I've been struck by the varying ways other cancer survivors handle their challenge. I've often seen how those who give up have poorer outcomes. I've seen those with aggressive/terminal cancer maintain their personal strength and dignity to the very end. I've witnessed upbeat, positive survivor personalities outgun their cancer.

For a while, I wanted to title this book *The Beauty of Cancer*, until my melanoma buddies convinced me it was too provocative. There is no beauty in cancer, they warned me. Yet I kept seeing beautiful people with touching stories enduring cancer with grace and admirable skill.

This ugly, terrifying disease produces amazing gifts of love, hope and spirit that inspire. That's a beautiful thing.

With love & hope,

Bob Heffernan
New Milford, Connecticut

RVH55@aol.com